MANUAL FOR LIVING

A USER'S GUIDE TO THE MEANING OF LIFE

CONNECTION

Also by the Author

Book One—*REALITY*

Book Two—*CONNECTION*

Book Three—*PURPOSE* (Coming Soon)

Praise for *Manual For Living*

"Loving this guide of understanding how to live. I am loving this guide and it will sit next to my bibles! Everyone interested in living should have this guide! Your words for me are food for the soul, my pot of gold. It validates my new self and provides good sound direction for me to tap back inside of me and be who I was meant to be from birth."

~ Helen F. Jones, Illinois

"This book could not have been more appropriate and needed. This gift you sent out to the world will forever be greeted with grateful and loving arms. Thank you for everything but most of all the keys."

~ Claudia Remón, California

"Thank you for sending me your book and all I can say is WOW as well! I can hardly put it down … Simplistic, thought provoking, profound and inspired are just a few of the words that come to mind. I KNOW this will be one of my manuals for living that I will wear out! Thank you and abundant blessings to you!"

~ Melissa Monahan, Arizona

"Here is your reality bible. You need to get it … your book hits a home run."

~ Rob Kingsbury, Total Health Radio, 1510AM

"Your book is my favorite book I have read in ages. You have done a justice to us all by writing it."

~ Steve Kovacs, Radio Show Host

"It is a beautiful testament to life and living. A book to help one reach his greatest potential and grasp his dreams."

~ A Novel Source

"A direction in life is all some people need … a two-time cancer survivor's plea to his readers to live their life to the fullest using the advice within. Stating the power of family, love, peace, changing one's life for the better and being prepared for death, he has much to help readers fully embrace life. *Manual for Living* is a read that should be fully embraced by those who have lost their way."

~ Midwest Book Review

"*Manual For Living* gives you valuable insight necessary to enhance and enrich your life bringing you closer to fulfillment and true happiness. *Manual for Living* is full of wisdom to help you find your way. Every page is filled with human emotion about life, death, and everything in between. The writing is sharp and observant."

~ TCM Reviews

"My teacher appeared when I picked up the *Manual for Living*! I have been searching for inner peace my whole life. I got great comfort and many questions answered from the *Manual for Living*."

~ Kim Gerulatt, Texas

"If everyone on this planet could have only one book, the *Manual for Living* would be my recommendation. Author, Seth David Chernoff carefully, concisely and accurately takes his reader on a step- by- step approach to the "art" of living . . . filled with dynamic insight and practical recommendations on how to change our lives for the better. Highly recommended!"

~ Shirley Roe, Allbooks Review

"The *Manual for Living* by Seth David Chernoff is a book special to me. I want to make its words a part of my life. It is spiritually remaking my life along with my Holy Bible. If you have the chance to pick up this gold mine to read, please do. It is saving me from wasting more time in my life. It is saving me from the fear of death. It is helping me in so many ways."

~ Book Review, Read With Tea

"A timeless wisdom that is more relevant these days than ever before."

~ Book Review, Andy Lloyd

"*Manual For Living* is more than that: it is a window to a fresh, new, hopeful vision for what it means to be human. Read it slowly, and feel the world shift inside you. A unique blend of practical and spiritual wisdom."

~ Mark Gerzon, Bestselling Author

"*Manual For Living* is a guide to finding balance and reconnecting with your spirit. I have to admit that I was happier after reading *Manual For Living*. It showed me that there were simple moments of happiness that I had missed along the way. I'd recommend this book to everyone."

~ Luxury Reading

MANUAL FOR LIVING

A USER'S GUIDE TO THE MEANING OF LIFE

CONNECTION

SETH DAVID CHERNOFF

SPIRIT SCOPE PUBLISHING

Spirit Scope Publishing
6525 Gunpark Drive, Suite 370-249
Boulder, CO 80301
www.SpiritScope.com
Books@SpiritScope.com

Library of Congress Cataloging-in-Publication Data
Chernoff, Seth David
Manual for Living: Connection, a User's Guide to the Meaning of Life / by Seth David Chernoff
p. cm.
ISBN: 978-1-937215-00-2

1. Spirituality 2. Mind, Body & Spirit I. Title

Library of Congress Control Number: 2011908210

First Edition

Author Website: www.SethChernoff.com
Book Website: www.ManualForLiving.com

For Eli
Live your truth & follow your heart.

Dedicated to my queen,
our beautiful boys,
my parents, my brother,
and you.

Welcome to CONNECTION

Welcome to Book Two in the *Manual For Living* series. Although the series was written over the course of 10 years, starting in 2000, its contents are a far greater compilation.

I have experienced my full share of obstacles over the course of my life, including cancers, financial issues, legal challenges, chronic physical pain, family trauma, death, emotional strife, and on and on . . . but does it matter? Does that make me any different than you?

We all have our own challenges and are each faced with the obstacles that teach, guide, and give us the opportunity to find true happiness and fulfillment. It is up to each of us individually to listen to our inner truth, follow our path, and discover our true purpose in life. Belief without conscious choice is life on autopilot, on someone else's rules, lacking intentional engagement. It is our duty to engage and to question.

I wish you the very best on your journey, and remember—I wrote this book for you.

With love and blessings,

— Seth David Chernoff

Contents

Prologue

Like many, as a child I was gifted with numerous insights and understandings, yet I spent decades ignoring my inner wisdom and truth, only to stumble and fall over and over again. This was as much the result of inner turmoil as external mayhem. I have been challenged spiritually, intellectually, emotionally and physically; when I clearly could handle no more, the havoc and opportunity only grew larger. Sometimes I allowed myself to become engulfed by extreme pain and suffering, but only in direct proportion to my ignorance and disregard for my own truth and path in life.

In the end, my life has been exhilarating and spectacular in many ways, with every experience granting me the opportunity to grow, to learn, and to evolve. I have survived cancer on two separate occasions, lived with chronic headaches every single day of my life since I was five-years-old, and experienced extreme physical pain so unbearable that I became physically sick and temporarily paralyzed. As traumatic as the physical pain was, it paled in comparison to the mental, emotional and spiritual growth I was afforded through this and countless other opportunities for growth.

~ Through hardship came strength, and as a result of pain I found joy. Through suffering came gratitude, and by letting go I found my path and purpose in life.

I have experienced the fullness of so much of life—the magnificence and the betrayal, true happiness and heartbreaking sadness, sickness and health, life and death, and true love. I have searched everywhere for the answers. But I eventually realized that the guidance I desired was actually here for me all along, not from outside myself, but from within. It was then that I found my truth and my purpose in life.

> ~ We each have a distinct path and purpose in life, a destiny as unique as our own fingerprints or DNA structure, yet we often live lives of petty obscurity and quiet desperation, ignoring our truth and our path, choosing to blame others instead of taking responsibility for our own choices.

Instead of receiving true happiness, love, and fulfillment, we experience it through a commitment to serve others and to find excellence in life. What if you really were in control of your life? What if you accepted that your current state of affairs was entirely the result of the choices you've made and the actions you've taken? What if you acknowledged that the present condition of your home, the quality of your relationships, your fulfillment at work, the size of your bank account, and the level of happiness you felt inside were entirely the result of all of the decisions you've made throughout your entire life? What if you stopped giving away your power and, instead, invested your time and energy in the creation of your life in exactly the form and manner you desired?

> ~ What if this book could help you find happiness, fulfillment, and love?

In life we often are forced to learn our lessons the hard way— through trial and tribulation, pain and suffering, failure and defeat. What if it didn't have to be that way? What if we could learn through others, by listening to the knowledge and wisdom of those who have travelled the road before us? What if we listened to our own truth and followed our inner guidance? We can alter and advance our consciousness in respect to all that we believe to be true. Take advantage of this information, as it is the culmination of a life lived through growth, dedication, and purpose.

A healthy skepticism is crucial to navigating the life-path before us and eventually discovering our truth and finding our inner voice. I ask you simply to try this on, take it as your own: Give your life a chance to become everything you choose it to be, everything you imagine it to be. Every chapter in this book has the possibility of enhancing your life, improving your relationships, deepening your understanding, and bringing you closer to true happiness and fulfillment.

- Don't expect that someone else will step in to fulfill the purpose you neglect, the path you disregard. Life is far too short, and your life is far too important.

Don't sacrifice your truth or your values. Each of us has a special place within this world, and it is our prerogative to find that purpose and fulfill it with every morsel of our being. The loss of a life is not nearly as devastating as the loss of what could have been, of the dreams left unfulfilled, and lingering passions undiscovered. This is not a book about religion; it is a book about life for those who choose to grow, who desire a more fulfilled life, and who accept that we are only as magnificent as we choose to be in this moment. This book is a reflection of my personal path in life, and I hope you will find it useful as you navigate your own.

Introduction

- How do we fully engage with that which lies dormant within us?
- What are we afraid to lose?

THE *MANUAL FOR LIVING* IS A USER'S GUIDE TO THE MEANING of life; it is a guidebook to balance and connection, intimacy and relationship, peace and love, evolution and fulfillment. What we desire cannot be "obtained," for it can only be experienced—the result of a life of commitment and service. Can we achieve lasting happiness? Can we find fulfillment or obtain true love? What exactly is a spiritual life, an inspirational life, a fulfilled life? What really is possible in life? Can we have it all?

The *Manual* will help you find clarity and assist you with connecting to your inner guidance—thus opening the gateway to an intentional life—a chosen life that is joyful and fulfilled. Few people on Earth possess the answers to life's simplest questions because in truth, answers are granted only to those with literacy in a language all their own.

- In life, answers often result only in further inquiry; the meaning we seek is found in the journey itself.

Inquiry and curiosity become the lifeblood of the living—the keys to assist us in our personal journey. We stay the course, learning through our environment and life experiences, challenges and opportunities. An individual's inquiry may actually safeguard against the very answers he or she seeks; the questions themselves being an indicator of the quasi-destination. We journey through the spiral of human evolution toward an existence of contemplation, verbalization, connection, contribution, service, fulfillment, and happiness.

The answer to life's meaning is different for every one of us and dwells somewhere deep within the epicenter of our being. We are in control of our heart, mind, and soul, and therein resides the core truth of existence. In large part, we are all identical, sharing similar core needs, wants, and desires. Inevitably, we will struggle with the same core issues and challenges. The greatest commonality of all humanity is that of life itself and its finality.

- The *Manual's* purpose is to help you find true happiness, understand why you are here, and discover your true purpose in life.

Challenge your beliefs and assumptions, and find your inner voice and truth in the process. Create the life you've always wanted by overcoming the obstacles before you, finding courage in the face of fear or adversity. Find the joy and magnificence in all things, and discover a new level of gratitude for everything that you have been given. Learn how to be fully in the moment and to let go of everything that stands in your way. Ease your pain, suffering, and struggle while embracing and overcoming the lessons before you. Encounter true balance, eternal happiness, and a powerful connection to your source. Learn to coexist and to function successfully on this physical plane without scarifying your spiritual core.

- Find true happiness on your path, and achieve everything you believe is possible.

The *Manual* is a practical guide to the hidden truths in life so you can better understand why we do what we do and live the way we live. Realize the basic truths to life and learn pearls of wisdom to guide your way. Understand the game of life and the role we play, individually and collectively, as physical and spiritual beings of service to the greater good of humankind. Discover answers to life's most troubling questions and the meaning behind our eternal search. Allow yourself to fully experience your spiritual journey of enthusiastic selflessness and the pride in giving, focusing your attention and manifesting your reality through continuous evolution.

> We all have much in common, yet we often feel so distant from one another.

In truth, we are all one in the same, regardless of intellect, age, race, creed, or dialect. No matter how much we contest this truth, there is little difference between us except how we have chosen to experience this lifetime. Life seems easier when we live as turtles, hiding in the shadows and emerging to seek nourishment, prosperity, and fulfillment, only to retreat into the protection of our shell when we realize that what we seek cannot be found outside ourselves. Seldom are rewards granted to those who hide from the world and its associated challenges and opportunities.

> Opportunities are endless when we choose to take risks and become present in our life.

This *Manual* is here to assist you in understanding and choosing a life fulfilled over a life of mediocrity, desperation, pettiness, or even worse, no life at all. When life is amazing, fulfilling, and spectacular, this *Manual* may gather dust; however, when you are faced with hurdles, challenges, and pain, it may help you persevere and be of service to those who await your guidance. The *Manual For Living* is a guide to support all beings in truth; to help us turn toward courage, honesty, integrity, and love; and to make conscious decisions that will ultimately guide us to true happiness and fulfillment.

> Whether our path is direct or circuitous, our destinations are constant; the eternal continuance of time combines with the temporal aspect of our physical existence.

Note to Reader

For the sake of clarity, I have chosen to use terms such as "Higher Consciousness," "Universe," "Spirit," and "God" within the pages of this book to describe the one all-encompassing entity, the guiding power within us all. The spiritual being within and around each of us is the energy to which we grant so many names and even greater responsibility.

Please note that this book is **not** designed to be read from cover to cover. In fact, you may find it most useful reading it one section at a time. When you require guidance, simply choose a chapter from the table of contents or take a full breath and randomly open the book. You may find yourself pleasantly surprised by the relevancy of the information you discover. Some of this information might be obscure or multifaceted, so take your time and give your mind, heart, and soul the opportunity to process what is being shared.

Enjoy!

Connection

Why do we isolate ourselves from those we love?

Why do we underestimate the power of connection?

Does everyone have a soulmate?

Can we ever fully accept human atrocity?

True Connection

A man travels the world over in search of what he needs
and returns home to find it.
—George Moore

- Do we ever really get to know another person?
- Do we ever take the time and effort required to truly understand ourselves?
- Are we able to let down our guard, our defenses, and our agenda to open our heart and truly connect with another?

CONNECTION IS MORE THAN CONVERSATION. IT REQUIRES true engagement, asking the appropriate questions, inquiring from our soul to truly understand the nature of another. There is some form of connection that occurs through observation, but an intimate engagement requires openness and is gauged by our ability to reach deep within our soul in order to connect to another.

- We forget that life is so quickly over and that living in the moment does not allow time for regret.

We only ever live in the present moment; and it is in that moment that we can have anything we desire. Ever so quickly we grow old, our kids grow up, our lives transform, and what we appreciate and enjoy within one moment may be entirely different within the next. Connection must be recreated in every moment, in every interchange, for we are able to bridge but not carry a connection of the past into the present. Our memory can only carry past moments into the present as a reflection of our selective recall.

> ⁓ Connection is not a task that can be completed; it is a way of being, a philosophy of living.

We look with our eyes, but do we seek with our soul? By looking with our eyes, we will see exactly what we expect to see within our reality: our perceptions and our pre-conceived notions. By looking with our soul, we have the opportunity to experience the soul of another. True connection is much more than simply building relationships or spending time with one another. True connection is not a function of the quantity of time we spend together, but purely the *quality* of our time. Connection can happen in an instant, in a flash, in a fraction of a moment, even without any words being spoken. Connection is not always something felt equally by both parties because we each bring to the moment a reflection of our own experiences and our own beliefs.

> ⁓ True connection requires openness from within, a nakedness of our soul, an exposition of vulnerability.

In life, we mentally understand that it is not our accumulations, our job titles, or our intellectual capacity that determines the quality of life. It is the closeness through which we live our life, through our heart, through our soul. We express our connection to source and our ability to intimately and honestly connect to those around us on a moment-by-moment basis.

~ In this reality, nothing really matters save the intimate connection we maintain with ourselves, our source, and with those around us.

Connection & Interchange

Talking is like playing on the harp;
there is as much in laying the hands on the strings
to stop their vibration
as in twanging them to bring out their music.
—Oliver Wendell Holmes

- Why do we feel drained or even exhausted when interacting with certain people, performing certain activities, or spending time in certain locations?
- Why do we have a hard time finding the right people to connect with—those who share our passions, our beliefs and our dreams?

In every connection and in every interchange, we give and receive energy on a number of conscious and unconscious levels. We give of ourselves and of our world, and we even share the very core energy that creates our life force. In doing this, we often absorb the reality of others and our external environment, whether positive or negative, while directly contributing to the adaptations of our inner environment, or our "invironment." We often feel exhausted, drained and worn out when partaking in certain activities, spending time with certain people, or even when traveling to certain cities. Some people, groups and locations have an incredible knack for extracting our life force, like a vacuum, often without our conscious consent or knowledge.

> ~ We must be conscious not only of that which we give, but also of that which we allow our bodies to receive, for we are far from invincible and must safeguard our energy.

Often the cause of a one-sided or detrimental relationship, such as an abusive parent, spouse, or friend, is readily apparent. Separating ourselves from an abusive person is not a sign of weakness but rather of strength; it is not giving up but setting boundaries. It is not failure but growth, development and evolution. We often think unkindly of ourselves when we choose to separate from those who are destructive in nature to ourselves or those who we love. On the contrary, by making conscious decisions toward our own health and growth, we protect ourselves and our loved ones.

> ~ We become stronger by finding clarity within ourselves, thereby giving us the courage and strength to live our own truth.

People and experiences are often presented to assist us in understanding what we see, feel, hear or sense—even that which we must disregard or are unable to accept. By following our soul's destined path, we are able to feel confident about our decisions, consciously or otherwise, whether independently or with the help of others. Sometimes the mere acknowledgement of a situation provides the stimulus for it to transform into a positive interchange. Other times we must clean up our own mess, which provides the opportunity to absorb every aspect of development available to us in that particular moment. We go about our lives, attempting to make the most of every moment while experiencing the consequences or realities of every experience whether by choice or in denial, but generally the latter. Our world is frequently perceived as overwhelming, with too many choices and not nearly enough time, and we often complain of boredom when in reality we are afraid to live our life, to follow our truth.

- In this moment, we currently posses only a fraction of the resources necessary to complete or obtain everything we desire, whether it be time, money, energy, effort, or even commitment and focus; but over time we will obtain everything we require.

As conscious and participatory social creatures, it is our conscious selection that allows us to associate with those around us who share our passion, belief, and understanding. By connecting to others committed to empowerment and evolution, we give and receive in a method and manner that supports and fulfills our goals and dreams of a life supported in greatness, purpose and understanding. We are not so different all of us. We inherently share a belief structure that, when engaged, has the potential to transform this reality into one of connection and peace, learning and evolution, love and joy.

Isolationism & Independence

The Constitution only guarantees
the American people the right to pursue happiness.
You have to catch it yourself.
—Benjamin Franklin

- Why do we isolate ourselves from those we love?
- Why does money have a tendency to pull us away from society and not closer to it?
- Why do we underestimate the power of connection?

AS A SOCIETY, WHEN WE INCREASE OUR AFFLUENCE, WE HAVE a tendency to pull farther away from society. Additional wealth begets a larger house on more land, a longer driveway, and a bigger gate. We isolate ourselves with affluence while the poorest among us live in close-knit communities sharing, where possible, the core needs of society—including food, time, space, and energy. We have become a society that doesn't talk to our neighbors, and for that matter, we may rarely even converse with our children.

- We drive our fancy cars into the garage, shut the door, and enter the privacy of our home without a moment given to connect with those in our own community.

Technology has a large role to play in our secluded nature. Unfortunately, we have isolated ourselves through our addictions to the telephone, e-mail, caller ID, voice mail, Facebook, Twitter, etc. We must ensure that technology does not get in the way of our connection to one another, for that connection is the most important thing in this world. We cannot replace humanity with technology. We used to have more interchange with our neighbors when we had fewer garages; our houses were closer to each other; we didn't have all of the distractions of technology, and it seemed that we as a society fostered our connections.

- In life, we strive for connection with one another. And yet when we achieve a higher level of societal success, we pull away from that very connection—one that fills the human spirit and helps provide the substance to a life that often feels less than fulfilling.

Why have we become so isolated? Why do we feel the need to disassociate from one another? As we enrich ourselves, we react in a manner that is contrary to human nature. Financial health cannot create the connection we seek, for what we desire can only be fulfilled from within ourselves, and only by ourselves, as a result of the choices we make in every moment. Community is everything in life. We are a society of interdependency, so intertwined in resources, in evolution, and in life itself.

- We underestimate the power of connection, something as essential to human nature as the air we breathe and the water we drink.

Recurring Soul Connections

The language of friendship is not words but meanings.
—Henry David Thoreau

- What is the divine significance of the people with whom we interact?
- What exactly is a soulmate? Does everybody have one? Can we have more than one?
- Why do we feel naturally comfortable with certain people, and not with others?
- Is it possible to reconnect with acquaintances from previous lifetimes?

WE MOVE THROUGH LIFE CONNECTING AND RECONNECTING with other similar traveling souls, all of us trying to find our way. We make subtle connections with people all around us as we progress through life. Little do we fully accept that the man at the deli who smiles at us, the woman who sits behind us at the office, or the boy next door who delivers our newspaper are all actors in our soul's entourage, surpassing many lifetimes and endless experiences. The soul is drawn to the familiar, whether places, people, or even the subtle realities within and around us. We associate with those people with whom we feel kinship and connection.

- Is it possible that those with whom we associate, whether family members, friends or associates, are people we've known from previous lifetimes?

We often turn a blind eye to the spiritual realities of our existence, as it's easier to ignore the truth and believe only in our manifested physical reality. As difficult as it is to see the truth within ourselves, every day children come into this world, bringing with them a close and intimate connection to their higher selves, to their spirit. Merely by their recency, they enter this world with a stronger connection to the spirit world. These children, sometimes called "indigo children," "star children," "crystal children," or "rainbow children," are able to clearly associate with and easily recognize those with whom they feel comfortable as a result of their previous experiences. We see children who recognize other offspring and create an instant kinship, a connection so profound that it cannot be explained by our common language.

- Our soulmates come in a wide range of forms, but the manner in which our lives interconnect provides no guarantee of connection.

By virtue of the various dimensions of time and space, the prospect of crossing paths with a soulmate is simply far beyond our mind's comprehension. Merely having and locating a soulmate does not entitle nor guarantee us a lifetime of connection and happiness; it simply allows us to locate sanctity in reconnection. The connections with those around us occur in manners beyond our intellect, and we are left to merely trust in the vast interconnectedness of our society at large.

~ We must remember that as a society, our connection is deeper than can be conceptualized. As a result, expressing a genuine kindness to everyone pays in more ways than we can imagine.

Supportive Connection

If God has created us in His image,
we have more than returned the compliment.
—Voltaire

- Why do we suffer?
- In a world where Spirit or God is the proposed centerpiece, how can we accept human atrocity, however large or small?
- As a global community, are we able to evolve beyond our seeming disregard for humanity?

WE ARE NOT ALONE AS WE STRUGGLE TO UNDERSTAND THE significance of the Universe and why it appears to wreak havoc with our reality. We pray or hope—every one of us in our own way—for a better world. Yet it often appears that our world doesn't really improve. It appears to digress into violence and mistrust as our communal evolution is stunted by the ignorance of a vocal minority. We see the incredible advances of science and technology, our increased life span, the evolution of Western medicine, a space station circling our planet, and the magnificent creature comforts we appreciate as natural elements of our existence.

- At the same time we have poisoned our environment, decreased the quality of our foods, overpopulated our world, and we continue to create greater income disparity.

We seem to take a huge step forward in many respects, but at the same time, we have taken a large step backward—as witnessed by world events of continual genocide, child trafficking, and new diseases. We win some battles and yet even more atrocities surface from areas never expected. We can create a supportive environment, in our community and in our world, in which each of us has the space to contribute.

- We have not only a desire to be liked but to contribute in service and support to those we love, whether in recovering from a bad day or a traumatic event.

Our generosity in helping others succeed comes back to us many times over. Our commitment to create a certain level of subsistence for all of society, to provide for the needs of others, will create a healthier community overall, one of support and co-creation. These concepts are not superficial; they are the inevitable outcome of combining our energies into one of focus and positive co-existence, feeding our innate desire to co-exist and feel a sense of belonging.

- The destiny of our society is reflected in the image we collectively hold of ourselves, which must evolve as we do individually.

We can love everyone; we can appreciate everyone. We may express our feelings differently, yet we are all here to love and be loved. In that context, it is difficult to hold disparaging feelings toward anyone. If we live from our heart, we can see the magnificence in each and every one of us, the beauty all around us, and we can appreciate the deep interconnectedness that we all share. If we realize that we all need to belong, to be a contributing member of a greater community, perhaps we will realize that what we share outweighs our differences.

- It is what we have in common that is the basis for the connection we require.

We may not perceive our world to evolve as quickly or in the manner we would like, but it is our contributions that determine the quality of our existence. The evolution of our global community requires the involvement of each and every one of us. We should not focus on changing the thoughts of others, but our own.

- We should not focus on forcing others to become who we want them to be, but on becoming the person we know ourselves to be.

We must lead by example for that is truly the only way to impact change on a global scale. We must demonstrate and showcase the opportunity for greatness that exists within each and every one of us.

Conflict & Resolution

Harmony seldom makes a headline.
—Silas Bent

- Is conflict a natural aspect of the human dynamic?
- How can we live and grow in a society that both attracts and abhors conflict?
- Is confrontation required for the evolution of ourselves and our communities?

IN LIFE, THERE ARE THOSE OF US WHO SEEK AND EXPLOIT drama, finding value in exaggerating the realities of our lives. The existence of reality television, most talk shows and the news, is based upon our innate desire for life's drama. Success doesn't sell nearly as effectively as drama, and there are those who absolutely thrive on chaos, who need it as much as the air we breathe. These very same people can be found complaining about the drama in their own lives, the drama that they have worked so very hard to create.

- There is no reason to complain about our lives, for they are of our own creation. We are the only ones in control of the reality in which we live.

We have no right to complain about what we manifest when the end result is only increased drama. That is how a life of conflict and tribulations is manifested. A life of magic, joy, happiness, and love is one that we also create. Our external environment is a reflection of our internal environment, and as a result, we can blame no one for the realities of our existence—except for the person reflected in the mirror. We will not fulfill our desires by searching the globe, for what we desire must first be located within ourselves. Our outer life is a reflection of the world within; what we seek is what we are.

- We mustn't run away from our lives to attain what we desire. Avoidance and aversion only empower that which we abhor. The greatest opportunities for growth and evolution occur within our lives, not outside of them.

Life would be much easier and less conflicted if we all accepted and reminded ourselves that our paths are parallel, our challenges are equal in nature, and our final destination identical and irrefutable. Nobody wins or loses. The eternal battle of life has a guaranteed destination. We are left with the option of making decisions in light of that fact and in consideration of the inevitable. We have full freedom of choice to see what we choose to see, to experience what we choose to experience, and we have nobody to blame but ourselves for our faults and failures. When things aren't going right, we need to fix them, either from within or without, or our pain will continue.

- We will see whatever greatness exists in this world as a reflection of what we are able to experience within ourselves.

Communicate

Why do we feel all alone?

Is anything more important than connection?

Do we ever really understand another?

What do we need to let go of in order to connect with another?

Do we ever REALLY *listen?*

Communication Is Everything

The most important thing in communication
is to hear what isn't being said.
—Peter F. Drucker

- How much of our world is strained due to miscommunication?
- How many relationships are prematurely terminated due to misunderstandings?
- Do we underestimate the power of the spoken word?
- Why don't we think before we speak?

WE SORELY UNDERESTIMATE THE IMPORTANCE OF COMMUnication and its powerful effect on every facet of our lives. Conflict in society, wars, religious battles, and breakdowns in relationship can often be traced to communication problems, disagreements, or simply differences of opinion. The majority of the legal industry is based upon the extrapolation or even exploitation of communication issues. Holy wars, marital troubles, and even divorce can many times be traced back to core communication breakdowns or disagreements.

- Every interaction is based on communication, and it is our maturity and ability to stay true to our source that determines our ability to communicate efficiently and effectively.

What exactly is good and effective communication? The basis for quality communication in itself is extremely simple. We act with kindness and respect, speak honestly, and share our feelings openly and respectfully. We must be open to alternative perspectives while letting go of our agenda and any attachment to outcome. The brain has a propensity to manipulate our senses or rationalize our experiences and sensations, but our true feelings cannot be manipulated. We must look beyond our mind to our feelings, which are the real gauge of our truth.

- We must trust in the Universe that everything will work out exactly as it was destined, especially when connecting with our heart.

We have a tendency to be loathsome communicators, which can be partly attributed to our pace of life, the increasing demands on our time and attention, and the lack of focus and intention we place upon our communication. Our society is rife with false expectations and disappointment, often occurring when two parties aren't effectively communicating. We can be wound so tightly that the slightest inclination of something distrustful, unethical or hypothetically harmful to our reality puts us on the defensive. We become upset, angry, or disappointed, even before we have a chance to adequately process the information presented and respond appropriately. Unfortunately, we all pay a price for our miscommunication.

- We judge on a whim, question others' motives by default, and fail to clarify when issues arise.

The filters through which we listen allow for discretion or selective listening. We can be as precise as we choose with our communication, matching our emotions to our words, choosing our language with an exacting level of scrutiny. However, regardless of how much we attempt to control our words or actions, we have no control over how others interpret what they hear. We control who we choose to be in any given moment. We choose the actions we take and the words we speak. Everything else is left to the whim of another's reality.

> ~ We must have the clarity and confidence within ourselves to release any expected outcome from what is spoken; we must release that which we cannot control.

An immense level of greatness can be achieved in our lives merely by making a commitment to thoughtful and intentional communication. We can evolve consciously by being present in and around our lives, opening ourselves to meaningful and heart-felt connections, and doing our part to create a society of balance and respect.

Human Interaction

Biographies are but the clothes and buttons of the man—
the biography of the man himself cannot be written.
—Mark Twain

- Why are we so stubborn?
- Do we pretend to know more than those around us?
- Are we more knowledgeable? Do we have all the answers?
- Are we living a "destinational journey," whereby the journey itself is the destination we seek?

WE RELINQUISH EVERYTHING TO BECOME THE HUMBLE beings we really are, accepting that we know and comprehend very little in order to receive everything we desire. We empty our mind to open ourselves to the answers we seek. Is there a limit to what we can comprehend? Is there a correlation to what we claim to know versus what we are open to receive—whether mentally, emotionally or spiritually? The subtleties of experience allow us to perceive and experience continually in every interchange of our lives. Just as every human interaction has a place and purpose as part of our evolutionary process, so does every experience play a significant role in the reality we desire, create, and avoid.

- We fight from the power of our ego until we become resolute in all that we are not.

We talk about life as a journey and not a destination, but it is symbiotic, as the end reminds us that the destination is the journey. Our purpose for being, our path within this lifetime, and our soul's purpose encompass the journey itself and not simply the destination.

- If we can see life for the amusement it really is, the lessons of truth become the impetus for happiness and fulfillment—the eternal "destinational journey."

We are limited to the knowledge we maintain in our mind in any given moment and are unable to comprehend fully the full intricacies of the world in which we live. Within our soul, there is no limit to the knowledge that exists throughout our world. We can accept a superficial understanding of this reality, but the deeper we venture, the more mystifying it becomes. The coincidental destiny of the universe baffles even the smartest among us, and eventually we realize that it requires more than brainpower to feel, sense, and understand the full path of our existence.

- We are simple beings of truth and purpose, and it is our ability to follow what we know to be true in each moment that is the basis for our magnificent journey.

We must be patient and open to what the world has to offer and we must come from a place of acceptance and modesty in order to appreciate what we have yet to experience and learn. The only way to become our greatness is to stay open, welcome what the world has to offer, and trust in the Universe for what the world has to provide and for what we are here to bestow.

- While following our path in life, we must also harness the humility required to see and experience the truth in and around us.

Communication's Shelf-life

Speak when you are angry and
you will make the best speech you will ever regret.
—Laurence J. Peter

- Why do we often utter the most hurtful statements in times of duress?
- Why do we say things we don't really believe, often in an attempt to cause pain?
- When we apologize for our poor behavior, is it ever forgotten?

IT IS SO COMFORTABLE AND EFFORTLESS TO SPEAK THE TRUTH of the world expressed in the way we live our daily lives or through the feelings we share from our heart. As pure and kind as we attempt to be, we do not always maintain kindness within our mind; but we are unable to offer anything *but* kindness when we live through our heart and soul. Our mind has the propensity to rationalize or even talk us into certain feelings or experiences.

- We need to get beyond our mind and into the truth of our existence.

Every now and again, we get upset and speak with a pettiness of our mind that pierces the heart and punctures the soul—words never meant to be spoken aloud. After the fact, we may apologize and beg forgiveness from those we hurt, but the damage only disappears from our vision. The resulting wounds secrete at the least opportune moments as we are dragged into a regurgitation and resurgence of the past, reliving it again and again. Sometimes the damage is so deep that it severs the tendons of connection, tendons that through time can be repaired but may never fully heal.

- The memory of a wound lives on forever. It is possible to heal and ignore but impossible to forget, for the soul maintains perfect memory of all things.

Words themselves carry only part of the meaning we share in communication, for it is the comingling of our language, mannerisms, and emotions that formulate the impact and the resulting effect on the deep vibrations of connection. Conflict does have the potential to create closeness, for through conflict we have the opportunity to actually deepen our connection as the tendons of truth and spiritual connectivity actually become tighter. When two people are willing to open their hearts, invest in the relationship, and work through their challenges, the end result is often grander than either ever expected.

- The subtleties create our reality.

Practicing integrity in our communication is rarely easy, for it generally requires an uncanny commitment to conscious communication. It is a refined balance between the words we don't want to share but need to be spoken aloud, and the words we wish were never spoken that inflict only pain or hurt.

~ In the end, it is not how we act in a single moment that determines the greatness of our existence, but the overwhelming consistency within every moment of our lives.

We rarely forget the harsh words received from difficult interchanges with friends, parents or peers. We often carry our own scars from childhood well into our adult life. Children are often unable to clearly communicate their feelings, emotions and sensations, so it is our role as parents, teachers, and mentors to teach communication and to practice restraint as we diligently try to keep our youth's best interests in mind.

~ We may continually recreate the present moment anew, but we are always simultaneously in the shadow of the past and in the presence of the future.

Self-esteem requires a lifetime to create and only a moment to destroy. There is a temperance and permanence in all things.

Ignorant Beings

From the errors of others, a wise man corrects his own.
—Publilius Syrus

- Why are we so ignorant?
- How can we pretend we are intelligent beings of purpose yet act in ways that are ignorant and trite?
- Why can't we hear and accept the truth the first time?

AS HUMAN BEINGS, WE ARE BY OUR VERY NATURE IGNORANT. We want everything delivered to us on a silver platter without having to take responsibility for our thoughts, actions, or current situation. We hardly listen to others and rarely to ourselves. Many times it is our own judgment that stands in the way of the clarity we seek. We receive guidance in a multitude of coincidental manners and methods, and we get a glimpse of what we are meant to see and understand. We hear messages from our parents and choose independence over their wisdom. We hear the wisdom from our best friend but decide to walk the path of independence in order to fully experience the lesson. We hear the answers from our children, peers, neighbors, and still we refuse to acknowledge the truth.

~ We catch a glimpse of a television show, read a word in a newspaper, or eavesdrop on a random conversation in a restaurant, and suddenly we allow ourselves to accept the truth.

It is through a wide range of manners and methods that we gather information in order to fully understand our truth. Often we must walk through the experience ourselves, feeling the pain and surrounding emotions, in order to embrace and fully accept our truth. Why are we so stubborn that we must hear something over and over before we recognize it as the truth? Why aren't we more trusting and accepting of this Spirit-given life?

~ Why do we force ourselves to suffer before we allow ourselves to evolve?

Ignorance is fought with repetition—a key element of transformation and evolution. We ask for the answers and beg for the truth, but when we hear it, we ignore it as if it were lies. We come up with endless excuses as to why we aren't receiving the truth: There were too many distractions. It was said in the wrong tone of voice. The wrong words were used. The wrong person said it. But eventually we accept what we have heard as a truth. The Universe utilizes repetition as often as is necessary for the message to be clearly received. Whether or not the information is utilized is a different story altogether.

~ We can save ourselves much hardship by listening to the Universe the first time and trusting our intuition and inner truth.

When communicating to others, we often need to repeat ourselves to be heard over all the distractions. But even once it has finally been heard, we are still left with the potential of miscommunication—a side effect of the chaos and potential overwhelming nature of our world. Communication is the foundation of everything, and the evolution of our society as whole will require an advancement in the clarity of our communication and the strength of our connection.

~ Our life is the end result of pushing forward on our path and with our passion for the betterment of our communities—one moment at a time, one soul at a time.

Selective Language

By swallowing evil words unsaid,
no one has ever harmed his stomach.
—Winston Churchill

- When does what we say have no impact on what is heard or the subsequent reaction?
- Why are we such poor listeners?
- Do we rarely feel heard because we ourselves don't listen?
- Is there too much information coming at us?

WE ARE ONLY ABLE TO CONTROL WHAT IS SPOKEN AND THE supporting emotions, but cannot control what is received. As a result, often it is difficult to perceive whether a message has been accurately received. Words fly out of our mouth often without hesitation, so amongst the multitude of distractions around us, are our messages accurately received? Our language tool belt allows us the possibility of positively impacting our direct dynamic, but we can never be assured success in communication.

- In school, we are taught math, English, science, but what about authentic communication, listening to the feelings in our heart, and being honest with ourselves.

What we learn through childhood takes us only so far, and eventually we are dependent upon continuing education and lifelong learning for the expansion of our communication skills. We have an incredible selection of verbs, nouns, and adjectives to express our thoughts, feelings, and desires—but often instead of choosing our words with intention, we say whatever seems prevalent and relevant in any particular moment. Where we may often be lethargic in our communication, we regularly act or speak without thinking and inevitably jumble our verbiage or choose words with dual meanings, creating ambiguity and confusion. We intend to complement, yet the listener hears only criticism. We attempt to share from our heart, but our listener's pain becomes inflamed. We sit quietly and listen, but our partner feels neglected or ignored. Why is communication so complicated?

- When sharing our feelings, we may mistakenly choose words that create instant judgment from others, even when in our heart our intentions are pure.

Using expressions of blame as opposed to sharing our feelings often ends up damaging the very connection we seek to repair. As individuals searching for a deepening of connection through communication, we struggle with the appropriate language. Often we are guided to disregard the words reeling in our mind for the feelings we experience in our heart. We discover that our true intention can never be spoken—it can only be felt. We cannot persuade another if they do not feel in their heart the direct connection between what is felt and what is spoken.

- As much as we attempt to be in the moment, communication is dependent upon the beliefs, history, and life experience of each party, as these are the filters through which everything is communicated and received.

Language and communication have become second nature, especially as our society depends increasingly upon long distance communication through technology. As we expand our distance-based interactions, the quality of communication tends to deteriorate. As we make assumptions as to what others will understand, exact word selection becomes essential as true emotion is more difficult for long-distance recipients to decipher.

- Irrespective of whether our communication is accurately received, through communication we often discover our own clarity.

There are so many levels of communication that expand far beyond the words spoken, for our overly analytical minds may find one element inconsistent and discredit the entire interchange. Far beyond the words spoken, we rely upon the emotions, sensations, and feelings to provide us with a gauge of the message's accuracy or sincerity. When in a state of peace, following our heart rarely results in misunderstanding. Disagreement, debate, and argument are elements of the mind that can't compete with the truth of the heart. We must pay greater attention to the trite interactions because even though they may seem insignificant at the time, their impact is immeasurable.

- We must focus on clarity, speak from our heart, and use clear intention.

We must impart communication in a method that has the best chance of being clearly received by others. Our life of miscommunications and misgivings results in a world that is convoluted and a vision and focus that is clouded.

- Clarity in life and all our aspirations requires clarity in communication—with Spirit, with others, and with ourselves.

Disagreement

Do we really need to be "right"?

Are we wrong in our desire to be "right"?

Are there some who invite conflict into their lives?

Can we avoid conflict without sacrificing our beliefs?

Nobody Is Ever Right

Nobody stands taller than those willing to stand corrected.
—William Safire

- Why do we always have to be "right"?
- Must we prove everyone else wrong?
- Can we bring those we love closer to our heart while simultaneously pushing them away?
- Is it more important to be right than to have connection, to have a healthy relationship?

NO MATTER HOW RIGHT WE THINK WE ARE IN TIMES OF DISagreement, the shallowness that we harness in order to feel "right" isn't worth it. It doesn't matter if we are right or wrong because the goal and purpose of this existence is not dependent upon either. We can never be completely "right," for in that attempt we inevitably wrong the ones we love, and instead of creating connection, we generate distance. Even when we are right, especially in the context of a relationship, by fighting for what we believe to be the truth, we often end up losing what we truly desire.

- We need not advocate being "walked on," but rather walking the spiritual path with the understanding that connection is more important than our ego.

Even when we are correct in principle, a loss of connection can result. We may be accurate in our restatement of the facts, but the truth often turns out to be much deeper than what we initially ascertained. We experience a void of understanding when spending far too much time in the vicinity to the truth yet choosing ego over love.

- By attempting to be right, we will sacrifice not only our relationships, but our life itself, for the basis for our life is the connections we share.

By obsessing about the principle of a past experience, we will not only wrong another, but will live a long and painful death as we end up punishing only ourselves. Judgment will carry us to the grave faster than anything else, for freedom is only found in forgiveness. There is no "right" or "wrong," only our perception. Let's not blame our partner when, in truth, our physical senses may deceive us.

- What we see is not real. What we hear is not real. What we feel is not real. What we perceive is not real.

Our reality is not a function of our senses, but a function of our belief systems. Our senses and perceptions provide information that supports or detracts from that which we believe, which in turn provides us with the answer as to what is real and what is not. We cannot take everything at face value, for our perceptions are accurate only in relation to our experiences, thought process and belief system.

- Knowledge does not create wisdom; having all the right answers at the wrong time makes no one the wiser.

It is much easier to assume we are wrong to begin with than to attempt to be right and find out later that we were wrong. If we all assumed we were wrong and ended up being right, we would continually meet or exceed all of our expectations, resulting in a fulfilled existence and perhaps a deeper ongoing level of connection.

- If we threw away our need to be right, we could focus on the relationship, the true goal at hand, the connection and love that we all inherently desire and require.

What kind of world would we live in if we assumed that our partners were right, trusted their insights, and were confident that they would handle every situation perfectly? What if we assumed that it simply didn't matter what was right or wrong, but only what the feeling was, what the truth was behind the action? What if we accepted that every situation happened exactly as it was destined?

- Our goal in this lifetime is not to stake our claim, but to help manifest the connectedness in others that we innately seek within ourselves.

There is no right or wrong, only what actually happens and what we perceive happens. It doesn't matter if we do something right or wrong or according to the "plan," but merely that we do it at all, that we show up, take action, and consistently proceed along our path.

Disagreement Is Futile

The need to be right is the sign of a vulgar mind.
—Albert Camus

- Why do we disagree with each other?
- What is it we are trying to prove?
- If we have the right answer, does that mean we are right?
- Can we achieve more by simply admitting defeat?
- Is it better to be right or to be happy?

We must accept disagreements as a common side effect of healthy relationships, as a sign that two people care enough to communicate. In our society, we have a tendency to blame others for our happiness or lack thereof, when there is no blame to be made. In relationships, we can merely agree to disagree, and nobody is right or wrong.

- Blame and disagreement do nothing but create distance between us, separating us individually in a world that operates collectively.

By seeing beyond the places or areas where we may disagree, we have the potential to maintain a heart connection far beyond what can be comprehended by the pettiness of the mind. Within the world around us, we have the world within, and it is that inner world that has the potential to fulfill all of our dreams, fantasies, and even our nightmares.

> ~ Our world is our own, and all that matters is what we make of it in any given moment.

We can disengage with others to reconnect within. We can join others within their reality, or we can invite others into our personal world, but in the end our reality is ours alone to create. The problem or disconnect appears when the reality of the world is diametrically opposed to the reality in which we live. If we live a disparate life from that which we feel or believe, we live a lie. If we live in a world in which we disagree with its global purpose, we will feel disconnected and apart—unable to be united as one when we are many.

> ~ We live a life that has no value, no meaning, and no purpose when it is incongruent with our inner truth.

There are trite inconsistencies in life that we feel require our attention and even disagreement. But in regard to those whom we love, we should be able to agree in principle to almost anything. We don't have to agree on everything but by focusing on elements of agreement, we have the opportunity to share, deeply connect, and contribute to those around us. By focusing on agreement, we center on common ground, on a successful foundation for the present and the future. We have the opportunity to expand our individual reality to include a global vision for humanity's potential.

> ~ We can become part and contribute to the grander vision for humankind, for all that we hold dear, for our collective path and purpose, and for the evolution and fulfillment of our society at large.

Disagreement & Conflict

It is better to keep one's mouth shut and be thought a fool than to open it and resolve all doubt.
—Abraham Lincoln

- Why do some people avoid conflict while others seek it?
- Why do some believe that harmony is the basis for our existence and others find joy and satisfaction in fighting or arguing about anything and everything?
- Is it possible to disagree and at the same time find harmony in connection?

THERE IS NOTHING WRONG WITH DISAGREEMENT, FOR AS intentional and active beings in this world, we will never agree on everything. We are individuals entitled to our personal beliefs and understandings, which will evolve over the course of our existence. Together, the merging of our thought patterns and understanding create a far more powerful collection of morals and values by which to live. In a perfectly democratic society, the morals and values of the community itself would be based on those of the common majority. In our society, where our community is a conglomeration of minorities, there exists a mixture of the vocal minority, the power centers of government and the subtleties of societal evolution. As a result, it is impractical for everyone to agree with every decision or every belief pattern. We are independent thinkers, and through disagreement we proclaim our freethinking autonomy.

> Even in times of conflict, we must realize that we cannot fight every battle nor win every war.

We must consciously and distinctively choose the battles worthy of our effort and intention. We must choose battles worth winning, or at the very least, worthy of our commitment and contributions. We will not win every war, nor is our participation simply for the end result. Often simply by our presence we can achieve success on the smaller fronts, resulting in the true achievement we seek. In looking at the challenges before us, we must decide if facing this challenge will get us closer to or farther from that which we desire. If it is the latter, we are better off focusing our efforts in a different direction.

> There is nothing wrong with dissent or disagreement, for we generally dissent with people and about topics we care most deeply.

When total agreement is not an option, we can agree to disagree, respecting each other's opinions and moving forward. We can respect the continuity of existence whereby each of us has our own view of reality. We live in a society comprised of a multitude of lifestyles, views, beliefs, and opinions; and we may perceive them to be right or wrong, but in truth, who are we to determine if something is wrong or right? Every action, thought, or viewpoint can never be right or wrong; it simply *is*. It is through varying viewpoints that the perfect equilibrium of the universe is maintained.

- We can control only that which resonates from within our soul, from within our being. It is fruitless to try and change the belief system of another, for it cannot be done without their full and unwavering consent.

Disagreement is natural, expected, and a healthy aspect of a free society. Because we can rarely change another's mindset or perception of reality, we are left to agree whenever possible and respect each other's dissent for the remainder. We are here for connection and to be of service because at the end of the day, none of it really matters.

- It is our contributions within every moment that determine the greatness of our existence.

Communication Problems

Don't speak unless you can improve on the silence.
—Spanish Proverb

- How can people be best of friends for decades and then suddenly refuse to speak to each other?
- Why do some family members despise the thought of another?
- Are there people we refuse to communicate with for whatever reason?
- What is it about our language or society that invites communication problems?

COMMUNICATION BREAKDOWNS ARE RIFE IN OUR SOCIETY. Some blame the English language for its inconsistencies or inability to express specific feelings or particular details of a situation. Others blame our society for the type of connections fostered in school and in business or for the low expectations we have in regard to communication and relationships. Beyond the inherent inferior quality of our ongoing communication, we have a tendency to easily destroy quality connections over diminutive communication discrepancies. We can all blame some aspect of gender inequality, upbringing, manners, or even the respect we share for one another, but in the end what makes the difference is the quality of our communication.

> ~ Our relationships require a greater commitment to connection than what is commonly accepted, a greater level of clarity with regard to communication than is currently available.

Why are we so quick to write-off quality relationships over misinterpretations or missed expectations? Our lives are a reflection of our growth and evolution, and as human beings, mistakes are a natural aspect of our existence. Beyond forgiveness, we must have compassion and understanding for the plight of those around us. We must be open to the path that each of us follows and the misunderstandings that are natural elements of our world.

> ~ Communication is everything within our existence; it is how we relate and communicate to others, to ourselves, to our spirituality.

Communication is not only what comes out of our mouth, but what radiates from our being. Without communication, we are nothing, as we have nothing to give and nothing to receive. Every aspect of our reality is based in communication, in a sharing of ourselves and a reception of what is available for us to receive. Communication is the largest boundary to human connection and the most significant element of conflict within our communities. We are very poor communicators, rarely sharing that which we hold true to our hearts, and through selective giving, we offer only a fraction of ourselves to our greater world. We are dependent upon others to help us reflect upon the connections we share. By becoming better communicators, we instill in others the opportunity to do the same. We find deeper and more meaningful connections within ourselves and with others as we strive for honesty in all areas of our existence, beginning with the very communication we share with ourselves.

~ First and foremost, we must be honest with ourselves in order to create the connections that we require.

Judgment

Are we perfect?

Are our imperfections a reflection of our perfection?

Is our judgment of others a reflection of our lack of self-acceptance?

Is it possible to live without judgment; whether of ourselves or of those around us?

Can we ever truly love another if we don't love ourselves?

Non-linear Development

God has given you one face, and you make yourself another.
—William Shakespeare

- Is life perfect? Are we perfect?
- Were we perfect when we began this life? Why do we feel so imperfect now?
- Why is it so difficult to maintain love and connection to our source throughout our daily lives?
- Can we live in a manner that supports our path in life?
- How do we maintain our passion for life even when challenged?

THE RATE OF DEVELOPMENT IN LIFE IS NOT LINEAR; IT HAPpens in accordance with the path of life itself. It is most apparent in children in those moments when they appear incredibly mature, and moments later they are again infants experiencing the fullness of childhood. At times we are astounded by their truth, words coming from a source far beyond their years. Children can speak from their soul, perhaps due to a recency of entering this life that allows them to maintain a closer connection to their spirit than most. They often maintain a higher and stronger vibration. Most children are also not yet tainted with a belief system altered by our external environment or by the pain we incur in this physical life.

- We all enter this life with a perfect connection to our source. Over the years, that connection gets cloudy and complicated due to the day-to-day realities of our existence.

We have a tendency to separate from our source over the course of life. While we may maintain, we are unable to hold onto the connection to our source. So we often become attached to our physical possessions in lieu of the true connection we desire. As we grow and develop, we constantly seek deeper connections, more heartfelt exchanges, and a deeper connection to our source. Without conscious effort, those connections are more easily obtainable at the beginning and ending of life. Children without the impact and detriment of a lifetime of programming can often more easily share their truth, their inner knowing.

- As we move through life, we do not have to detach from our strength, from our source.

We don't have to accept this world for everything that it appears to be. We have the opportunity to walk our path and speak our truth without getting caught up in the pettiness of this world, for the world is ours for the making. Babies are born without hatred or anger; infants never intend to inflict pain or cause hardship. Babies enter this world as perfect beings intimately connected to their source, to their soul.

- As we move through life, we lose some of that connection, replacing it with anger, hatred, and even disgust.

We slowly separate and distance ourselves from our own soul connection as we immerse ourselves in the world before us. We must remember that we are spiritual beings here for a physical experience. We have the tendency to become attached to the physicality of the world around us while disregarding the most important aspects of our existence. Our culture thrives on trite physicality, and we tend to nurture superficial, even passionless connections. Our life is the perfect blending of the spiritual and the physical. Our connection to our own source is the most essential aspect of our existence, and we will spend our entire lives trying to find, maintain, and deepen our connection to it.

> ~ We must find the truth within ourselves and follow our individual life path and purpose, finding our true passion.

Our growth and evolution through childhood, adolescence, and adulthood is not linear, consistent, nor always predictable. Our emotional body may develop at a different rate than our physical or intellectual body. The evolutionary process is extremely complex, and the inner workings of the soul are far more intricate than we can imagine from this physical plane. Many in this world will develop intellectually but never emotionally, or physically but never mentally. We may experience development in all areas but regress in moments that confuse and surprise ourselves and those around us. We all are on our own path, utilizing the tools and skills available to create our destiny. It is that very connection to our source, to our soul, to the child within that fades as we fully enter our bodies and move through life, becoming focused primarily on our physicality and discounting our spirituality, thus preventing us from finding true happiness and lasting fulfillment.

> ~ As we age, our inner child is much more than a reflection of our inner desires.

The inner child represents the innocence within us all, the beauty and magnificence, the opportunity and possibility of our life. It is the child within that speaks to us and presents us with the opportunity to recenter ourselves for the journey ahead. The pure and present being within us grants us the potential for clarity amidst strife and confusion. It presents us with the grand vision, even as our eyes cloud with the physical reality before us. It is our soul that helps maintain our focus while we are pulled in endless directions, testing our focus, clarity, and resolve.

~ It is that which exists within us that allows us to operate outside of ourselves.

We have the opportunity to teach our children to hold onto their truth, giving them the chance to maintain their inner connection and spirituality throughout life. Just because we let go of our own connection and have spent our life working to reconnect to our inner truth doesn't mean that it needs to be this way for future generations. We don't have to learn everything the hard way.

~ We have the opportunity to transcend, to follow our truth, from the beginning of our life and throughout.

Relative Disdain

When there is no enemy within,
the enemies outside cannot hurt you.
—African Proverb

> ~ Why do we feel inconvenienced or uncomfortable by those who have less or appear to be less?
>
> ~ Why are those who struggle to conform treated with disdain and empathy when they are simply following their path just as we follow our own?

LOOKING THROUGH OUR SOCIETAL FILTERS, THERE ARE THOSE who appear less than adequate. There are those who seem to have less simply as a function of our communal norms. There are those who seem to struggle with conformity, who give the impression of a life of strife. Are they so different from us? Do they deserve to be treated differently than anyone else?

~ We are very quick to judge physical, mental or emotional appearance—but through our soul, we are only able to embrace.

Just because some choose a different path, does that make them *inadequate*? If they live off welfare and government sponsored support, does that make them any less of a human or spiritual being? How can we look down on them as lesser humans or as unworthy of the magnificence of the very world in which we live? Why shouldn't they frequent our restaurants or coffee shops, use our benches or walk on our sidewalks. We have become a new brand of segregationist, not only relation to a particular race or ethnicity, but in regard to an entire class of society, an entire demographic of our community.

> ~ Accepting and giving to those in need, to those who cannot provide for themselves, is not a requirement; rather it is an opportunity to accept all human beings equally, to embrace empathy, to experience compassion, and to be of service.

We should not underestimate the true potential or greatness of another. It is not our role to judge the quality of one's existence within this universe, for judging another only reflects a perceived superiority. The outward perception of one's success is only in relation to our societal norms.

> ~ True happiness and fulfillment is not something we can find outside of ourselves, but something that must be felt and experienced from within.

We should not judge another by their appearance, just as we cannot analyze a company by its office building or judge the quality of a friend by the type of vehicle they drive. We need to be open to the possibility that the guidance we desire may come from the most unusual people in the most unexpected of situations. There is always something to learn from those around us if we are open to receive that which is being provided.

> ~ Every being has tremendous power and potential, and their role in life is part of the intricate balance and synergy of the universe itself.

Our world is the conglomeration of every thing and every being within it, and it is through such diversity that our world has the potential for collective evolution.

Beyond Judgment

To know God's nature one would have to be God Himself.
—Joseph Albo

- Why do we judge one another? Is it possible to live *without* judgment?
- Why do our children grow to judge others and ourselves as we do?
- Can judgment be a good thing?
- Are we continually judged by a higher power, as if we were always on trial?

WE ARE A SOCIETY OF JUDGMENT—IT IS OUR WAY OF ANALYZing our place within this world, comparing the lives of others to our own. We judge our waiter on how our service was provided, and compensate them as such. We judge our children's teachers for their performance. We judge our parents for how we were raised and our children for their actions or lack thereof. Most importantly, we judge ourselves. Judgment is meant to be observation used to make rational decisions. However, we have a tendency to use judgment as the means for which we evaluate the *rightness* or *wrongness* of those around us as we attempt to determine their value or usefulness.

~ Who are we to determine the value of another human being?

Judgment in and of itself is an essential skill, helping us to evaluate and make decisions toward the betterment of our lives and those around us. Paying attention and assessing the world is a natural aspect of the human experience, but our form of judgment is often a form of self-manifested superiority in which we obsess and berate the actions of others.

~ God or Spirit does not punish or judge, classify or categorize based on any hierarchy; that appears to be a specialty of human beings.

Our judgment of others is a reflection of the way we judge ourselves. We punish ourselves for choosing the wrong things and making the wrong decisions. We ridicule ourselves for the choices we make that lead to the hardship in our lives. We so quickly forget that our imperfections are perfect for they represent the color in and around our lives. We are reflections of perfection, in the perfect place at the perfect time. There is a reason and purpose to all things, and to all things a purpose. Our society is designed to impose justice; however, in the greater sense, we have karma or the intrinsic balance of the universe to create equilibrium, to balance out the ebb and flow of the individual as it relates to our society.

~ We are not judged by God or Spirit, but there are natural consequences to the choices we make.

We are never punished. A challenging life holds with it the greatest of opportunities. Our world is in eternal and natural balance, a reflection of the perfect equilibrium of all things and all beings. Our soul finds balance not only in every moment, but throughout our lifetime. What we seek or desire in this moment is balanced by what we are able to discover, accept, and overcome in the next. What we miss in this moment is balanced by what we experience in the next, but eventually we hope to prevail over that which we avoided or evaded.

> ~ As we struggle with petty obscurity, all ails will absolve themselves in due time.

Let's be honest with ourselves; it's challenging not to be judgmental—it's contrary to our natural tendencies. It is difficult to look candidly at our own imperfections, to self-reflect, but we all too easily identify the faults of others. We see those who eat too much, don't exercise, and rarely take care of themselves and yet don't like the way they look or how they feel. We see people who are disrespectful or unkind to one another and then wonder why they continually feel disrespected. We see parents who fight with or berate each other or their children in one moment and complain about their lack of harmony, connection, or the separateness they experience with their children. We see friends who are selfish and self-centered and yet wonder why nobody seems to care about them. Is this reality, or are these simply our perceptions of reality, the distortions within our world that we use to justify our position? We will always see those less gallant than ourselves, but we are not here to compare ourselves to one another.

> ~ We can only compare our current self to the person we truly believe ourselves to be, the person of our highest good and greatest potential.

Judgment does serve a purpose; it allows us to objectively look at reality and our place within it to examine our opportunities for correction or improvement. But judgment is also an excuse we use to separate ourselves from those around us, a justification to disconnect. We are here to find ways to increase our connection to one another, and to create a more intimate and soulful connection to ourselves.

~ We must use our own sense of judgment to make good decisions for the betterment of ourselves and our communities, to continue to grow and evolve, to become the person we truly know ourselves to be.

Letting Go

How can we move forward while holding on to the past?

How do we move forward in life?

How can we be fully present in the moment while obsessing about the future?

How do we release those who have wronged us?

Can we ever fully forgive? Can we ever forget?

Letting Go

He is rich or poor according to what he is,
not according to what he has.
—Henry Ward Beecher

- Why do we get so attached to the physicality of this existence?
- What exactly are we holding onto?
- How do we attract what we desire without releasing the past?
- How can we fully appreciate the moment while fixating on the one to come?

THERE IS NO WAY TO ATTRACT WHAT WE DESIRE WHILE WE are suffering from that which we don't. Living a life of subsistence allows us to settle for a lesser career, relationship, home, or lifestyle without concern over its application or impact on our life of service or purpose. In order to fully open ourselves to what is available to us, we must be willing to relinquish everything that stands in the way of our path, our greatness, our happiness. We cannot attract a soulmate while struggling through a failing relationship. We cannot begin a new career while in service only to ourselves in a career of hedonism and personal exploitation.

- We must relinquish what stands in the way of everything we desire, a demonstrated action toward the intention and focus that we claim to maintain.

Intention without action is akin to designing a home without actually building it, writing a book without publishing it, setting the table and preparing the menu without actually making the dinner. In order to have what we desire, we must combine our clarity of focus with our moment-by-moment actions, an intention matched only by deed.

- We must be willing to give up everything we have in order to have the opportunity for what awaits us. We can't let fear prevent us from taking action —life is too short.

The laws of attraction and manifestation work hand in hand, a personal commitment to releasing everything that is standing in the way of our dreams, our desires. We must look long and hard at the life before us, the people around us, and the environment within which we live in order to ensure that everything is in alignment with our divine path. Our life can be everything that we desire, but it won't be without opportunities to grow and to serve. We can give those around us the opportunity to evolve with us, to grow with us, to step into their own greatness along with us.

- Beyond our own personal goals and desires, we must move forward in life together, to manifest collectively, to let go of all that stands in our way as a society, as a community.

Plan the work, work the plan, and then let go of your attachment to outcome. A plan is a form of strategic manifestation, a reality-based systematized plan for our future and our place within it. However, in God's realm and the realm of Spirit, we must release our plan for whatever the world has in store for us. Our hopes and dreams are a sedentary side benefit of a life of purpose, passion, and excellence. Our individual hopes for the future eventually dissolve when they are outside the scope of our path and purpose in life. By maintaining the focus and clarity we desire in life and by relinquishing all that stands in our way, we are able to attract all that we desire. We are unable to attract anything that exists outside the scope of our path in the life and the associated opportunities for growth that await us. We are given all that we require, but not always all that we desire, until we eventually realize that they are one in the same.

~ In life, everything is available to us if we can make the difficult decisions that give us the opportunity to have all that we desire.

Moving Forward

The soul becomes dyed with the color of its thoughts.
—Marcus Aurelius Antonius

- How do we move forward in life?
- Do we actually move forward, or are we inert as the world revolves around us?
- Why are some of us stuck in the same routine or constantly re-learning the same lesson?
- Why are we unable to see the answers to our own dilemmas when we can see the answers to others' with crystal clarity?

SOMETIMES IT FEELS LIKE WE ARE STUCK IN A RUT, IN A PATtern we cannot seem to alter no matter how hard we try. How do we move forward when it feels like our life is standing still? There are three core elements of moving beyond our current position into the manifestation of our dreams and achieving our goals of happiness and evolution: Live, love, and release. To begin, we must live life to the fullest, taking every opportunity to experience new things, overcome challenges, and to evolve into happier and healthier human beings. We should also love everything and everybody with all of our being, in every way imaginable, becoming an open channel for emotional connection and creating the space necessary to give and receive in the nature of love itself.

> ~ We have the opportunity to let go of the past, the future, and even our agenda of the present moment.

And finally, we need to let go of bad relationships, uninspiring clothes, and old furniture. Release bad habits, limiting beliefs, and restrictive thought patterns. By letting go of the old, we make space for the new. By getting rid of our old furnishings, we create the physical space for new furnishings to arrive into our life. By releasing an old relationship, there is space for a new one. Letting go is intricately tied to our ability to live and our capacity to love. Perhaps something is blocking our ability to truly love another, to fully feel and experience love—or perhaps something is preventing us from reaching our full potential.

> ~ We store our emotions and elements of the past within our cartilage, our bones, and our energy field.

In order to release those experiences that stand in the way of our greatness, mental commitment alone is not enough. To fully release the past or the emotions that stand between our true selves and our future, we must provide a physical release that propels a corresponding emotional release. Sometimes what appears to be an "accident" is actually a physical adjustment that triggers such a release—like falling, tripping, bumping into someone physically, or even a car accident. Otherwise we can utilize massage, yoga, Rolfing, or physical exercise to assist in releasing those blockages.

> ~ In order to allow the emotional release that we long for, a physical trigger or action of some sort is often required.

On our deathbed, we won't wonder why we had not been someone else, but rather why we did not achieve the fullness of ourselves. We all come to this world for a reason: to give, to learn, and to receive. True fulfillment comes in the merging of this trinity. Release, forgive, love, and be of service, constantly and incessantly, in order to accept, receive, and serve again. We have the opportunity to fulfill our dreams, accomplish our soul's intention for this life, and do our part to help our communities evolve and transcend.

- We are all unique and our path is ours and ours alone. We are here to follow and fulfill our path, regardless of the perceived obstacles before us.

Positive Present

If you want others to be happy, practice compassion.
If you want to be happy, practice compassion.
—Dalai Lama

- Why is it so hard to stay positive in times of strife or challenge?
- When faced with negative experiences, why is maintaining our natural positive outlook on life so challenging?
- Why is it hard to stay present for the moment?
- Can antidepressants or recreational drugs assist us in our quest for greatness?

OUR ATTITUDE DETERMINES OUR ABILITY TO SEE AND EXPERIENCE the beauty and magnificence of our world. Changing our attitude is easier said than done—and in some cases may seem impossible. Perhaps the difficulty is a side effect of the challenges we face or the imbalance in our education that focused on outer health over inner health. The problem could be the increased toxicity of our world, the reduction in nutrients in our food, or pure self-ignorance.

- Our level of happiness and fulfillment is directly related to our ability to experience the greatness and beauty within and around us.

We need to self-reflect, learn to listen, and let our inner compass guide our experiences toward the beauty in life. Medications and recreational drugs are available to assist us with a wide range of real or imagined ailments, including permanent or momentary depression, apathy, or even helplessness.

- Regardless of the excuse, we are responsible for the choices we make in our life.

Whether the result of denial or depression, we are obsessed with managing our moods through whatever manner allows us the greatest sovereignty in life. Medicine has evolved along with society, stepping forward as we have lost our ability to see what needs to be seen and the strength to face the challenges in our life. We have a tendency to become dependent on that which takes us out of reality, away from our pain.

- In truth, spirituality is not seeking consciousness but the conscious connection to our inner truth.

We embrace the solution to our ailments in the format of growth and understanding in order to live happy, successful, and purposeful lives. Naturally and physically, we ebb and flow with the changing seasons, bullied by the manifestations of our external environment. As we move through life, we adjust to the seasons, the weather, daily mood swings, paydays, holidays, global conflicts, and even personal misunderstandings—challenging our equilibrium, our balance, on life's emotional rollercoaster.

- As we evolve, we learn to control our emotional wellbeing from within, regardless of external circumstance.

We all need a stabilizer. Some use medication, and others might meditate. Some take prescription drugs, and others find stimulants of a more social nature. Some of us take walks in the wilderness; others sit quietly, pondering reality. We exercise freedom of choice in how we react to outside circumstance; however, the emotions that percolate are the result of varied experiences. We react to people, places, and even words that are spoken often with reckless abandon. Our reactions are often the result of our belief system and experiences combined with our current state of being. If we want to change our reactions, we need to change our inner programming. Our beliefs and perceptions keep us ensnared.

~ If you want to be happy—find your happiness. Freedom is ours to experience in every moment if only we would choose it.

Convoluted & Complicated

If you want to be happy, be.
—Leo Tolstoy

- Do we make our lives more complicated than they need to be?
- Why do we mask our true feelings?
- Why is it so hard to be honest with ourselves?
- Why do we surround ourselves with the wrong people?

BY OUR VERY NATURE, WE ARE COMPLEX INDIVIDUALS AND can be difficult to understand. We have a tendency to act in ways that mask our true intention, convoluted by emotions and a communication method that doesn't breed the love and connection we desire. We find ourselves trying to connect with those, who in times of strain and difficulty, exhibit passive-aggressive or simply belligerent behavior. We attempt to bond with some who are often rude, disrespectful, judgmental, insensitive, or utilize methods to cover their true feelings and avoid relaying what they really think, playing the so-called "game" of life.

We soon accept that these bitter and feeble acts are merely a front for the true feelings within each of us. Unfortunately, expressing our authentic feelings in life is more difficult than it seems, for we must start by being honest with ourselves. Beyond the clarity we maintain within, many times our feelings are misread for judgment, or we share them with people who don't appreciate our true feelings or our truth.

> ~ By understanding that the basis for human nature is heart-seated connection in our relationships with others, we open ourselves to that connection in our own lives.

Without knowing how others are going to react, we have no choice but to assume that they have the best of intentions, whether they are able to express them or not. We must seek and expect inherent goodness. Independently, we all require integrity in our relationships, and the connections we maintain within and to others define our level of integration in this world. We must strive to share every moment from our heart, thus inspiring others to do the same.

> ~ We must reach out and take the first step toward a deeper connection with others so they are encouraged to respond in kind.

The time of superfluous and platonic connection is gone; this is the time for intimacy within connection—not of a physical nature, but one that reaches beyond the sovereign intellect and into the realm of the heart and soul. We cannot wait for others to make an effort at the connection we desire; it is up to us to manifest exactly the reality we desire.

> ~ We fulfill our life by living and breathing the life of service we desire with ourselves and those around us.

Forgiveness

Is betrayal an inevitable aspect of this world?

Why is it so difficult to forgive?

Is it easier to ask for forgiveness than to forgive?

Can we ever forgive ourselves?

Deception & Betrayal

The man who acquires the ability
to take full possession of his own mind
may take possession of anything else
to which he is justly entitled.
—Andrew Carnegie

- Why do some steal to obtain what they desire?
- Do we *allow* ourselves to be betrayed, deceived, or taken advantage of?

IT IS AN UNFORTUNATE TRUTH THAT SOME PEOPLE CHOOSE TO lie, cheat, and steal to get what they desire. Some will do whatever is necessary to obtain what they covet. We cannot control the actions of another, only our reaction to it and whom we choose to be in the process. Everything that goes around does comes back around, for the karmic balance of the universe is enforced of its own volition. This intricate ebb and flow is a naturally progressing energy to which we may contribute but cannot control.

- Although we may feel hurt, revenge only distracts us from our love and our connection to source. Life is guaranteed perfect equilibrium.

When we meddle and manifest anger and hatred, we hurt only ourselves, for where our thoughts go, our energy will follow. Without forgiveness, we relive our pain and anger and allow ourselves to continually re-experience the hurt. As long as we continue to live in the reflection of a past experience, we give our energy away and remain powerless as we pout and ponder. Our paths are intricate and interlocking, and it is not for us to understand the spectacular or fundamental grand scheme of life, nor the inner workings that allow us to evolve as we progress through life. We are asked only to move ever closer to our Higher Consciousness, to continue with the life purpose we have been presented, and to make daily contributions to the greater good of humankind.

- In the end, our contributions directly affect the evolution of our greater communities and our universe as a whole.

How do we trust again once we have been betrayed? Once we have been hurt, we are often predisposed to be overly judgmental, which can cause us to miss out on the very opportunities presented to us. On the other hand, with experience we learn to tread softly in the murky water, taking baby steps as we move forward to overcome our pain. We do need to take responsibility for our actions, but we can only control whom we choose to be and the actions we take. We may learn the intricate balance between locking up our heart or wearing it on our sleeve. We learn to taste, sense, and feel the energy in and around us. As we mature and evolve, our sixth sense and powers of intuition become second nature, and we begin to read the inner workings of those who seek our guidance. We learn to see through the flair and false expressions to that which we perceive to be "real."

- We discover the heart behind the mind and the intention behind the front to see that which is truly requested and required of us.

Just as a fearless child discovers his boundaries by inflicting pain upon himself one too many times, betrayal is a natural and essential part of evolution, for it helps us to discover and implement our own boundaries. As we impart boundaries on others, we must impart those same boundaries on ourselves in order to stay on course and on purpose.

- We cannot control another's actions, only our reactions to them, which is where our true power and freedom exists.

We are amazing creatures in so many ways. Over the course of our path, we are presented many opportunities to trust and to be trustworthy. We also have the opportunity to be manipulated along the way in response to the actions we take and our awareness of our path. As unique individuals, we pave the path of our own destiny and express our own magnificence. It is through this expression that we have the opportunity to either follow the path of integrity and spiritual purity or follow a selfish, fear-based mentality, centered upon greed, hedonism, and momentary gratification. As we make choices, we share with our higher Spirit what we desire in our life and what we choose to attract to ourselves, as well. We *do* reap what we sow. While we cannot be responsible for the karma, lessons, or reality of another, we must be fully responsible for our own reactions, acceptance and ability to move on to what is deserving of our attention, respect, love, and guidance.

- At some point, others may attempt to deceive and betray us. In the end, our only recourse is to forgive, for that is the only tool that keeps us on our path.

We must communicate, stand up, and protect ourselves, but in the end we must forgive. Why would we allow someone to control our destiny, our ability to stay true to our path? There is perfect balance in all things, and it is not our job to punish others for the pettiness of their actions. There is a distinction between societal justice and karmic law, but in the end we must give our path and purpose our full attention. We have a responsibility to let go, love, and revel in the greatness of our existence. There is a reason for everything, and although we may not always understand the full intricacies of the pain we experience, we learn to appreciate and accept everything, regardless of our perceptions of the moment.

~ In the end, everything works out exactly as it was destined.

Hatred & Anger

Each of us is something of a schizophrenic personality, tragically divided against ourselves.
—Martin Luther King, Jr.

- Why is it so difficult to release that which stands in our way?
- Why is it so hard to truly forgive?
- Why are we so quick to anger, raise our blood pressure, and allow ourselves to enter an almost uncontrollable state of being?

HATRED IS OFTEN DEFINED AS AN EXTREME SENSE OF DIStaste or dislike, yet it is so powerful as to command action. We are then driven to change our environment, either to destroy or avoid the hated feeling or entity. How powerful must an emotion be to drive or force action within our lives? Are we that susceptible to outside influence that we allow it to become the source of change in our lives? Hatred holds a special place and role within our society. Not only is it the opposite of love, but we use the term hatred too carelessly, commonly referencing such a powerful emotion when in fact very few of the emotions we experience command any action whatsoever.

- We must face, conquer and overcome our hatred and fears, or they will control and eventually destroy us.

Hatred or fear within us exposes others to our hardship, forcing alterations in our life that are often made without our conscious consent. We often experience emotions or make decisions that actually stand in the way of our success and happiness. Hatred is a powerfully negative energy, one analogous to self-inflicting pain and is a direct result of things, beliefs, or people that we strongly dislike, despise, or fear.

- Hatred and fear are akin to cancers of the soul, for as long as we are exposed to them, they will spread and eventually manifest into a physical disease or ailment.

As energetic beings, we must not only allow the energy to flow freely through us, but we must have the strength to release those energies that clearly upset the natural ebb and flow of our own stream of consciousness. We walk down the street and avoid the homeless man who begs for coin. We hold our breath when we walk into a restaurant past the smokers gathered outside. We make adjustments throughout every moment in an attempt to find more enjoyment of the moment before us or to avoid that which we feel will bring the opposite.

- Hatred and anger are forms of ignorance, as is the blatant disregard for the beliefs of others, as is the unwillingness to change.

Fluidity and Flexibility

Holding on to anger is like grasping a hot coal
with the intent of throwing it at someone else;
you are the one who gets burned.
—Buddha

- Can we ever fully enjoy the moment if we are holding onto resentment from the past?
- Can we be loving and angry at the same time?
- How do we become more fluid and flexible?

FORGIVENESS IS WISDOM, AS IS FLEXIBILITY, OPENNESS, AND understanding. Flexibility, fluidity and going with the flow of the universe is how we survive. Our ability to relax in the moment allows us to survive; rigidity is our downfall. A baby is soft and supple; children appear to be almost made of rubber as they practically bounce off physical obstacles. In our elder years, our bones become brittle and frail, shattering with minimal impact. A living tree moves with the elements, swaying freely from side to side as the wind caresses its leaves and branches. A dead tree simply stands firm and rigid until it eventually breaks, cracks, and comes crashing down.

~ The greater the fluidity we are able to inject into our lives, the greater our ability to go with the flow, to follow our path and to learn from our mistakes.

The greater our flexibility in life, the greater our ability to be open and to listen and evolve. It is through our commitment to greatness that we become soft and supple from the inside out, a beacon of interest and learning. It is through our own elasticity that we can ebb and flow easily with life—releasing and forgiving those who stand in our way.

~ When we forgive, we transcend the pettiness around us and are able to focus on the greatness that lies before us.

Eventually hatred manifests as a physical, mental and spiritual disease. If we cannot forgive—it will eventually destroy us. We are all given the necessary tools and opportunities for forgiveness. By releasing those we feel may have wronged us and forgiving ourselves, we create the space for our own evolution. This understanding allows us to look forward, to move forward, and to fully experience the moment at hand.

~ Anger and resentment originate from our lower selves; everything good in our lives always resonates from our higher selves.

Hatred, pain, and suffering can never originate from our higher selves, for they are result of our lower functioning, a lower vibration. Our higher selves cannot judge or hate; our lower selves are incapable of love, compassion, or respect. Our higher selves cannot criticize, demean, ridicule or kill; our lower selves cannot truly care, experience empathy, or love. By acting with compassion and kindness, we live within our higher selves; we are closer to our source and are acting out the purpose of our existence. The more we are able to live through our higher selves, the more powerful our gift to the world, and the greater our ability to live the fullness of our existence.

- By releasing others we release ourselves, for we cannot create our freedom if we are dependent upon others for our happiness and success.

Any negative attachment we carry or maintain from the past hinders the success, evolution and fulfillment we obtain in the moment. By releasing any and all judgment of others, and by forgiving those we may have reason to abhor, we release ourselves to be present in the magnificence of the moment, to fully experience all that this life has to offer.

Forgive Yourself

Life can only be understood backwards,
but it must be lived forwards
—Søren Kierkegaard

- Why do we work so hard to find connection, yet find it so difficult to forgive?
- Why is it easier to apologize than to forgive those who apologize to us?
- Why is it easier to separate ourselves than to create closeness?

WE HAVE A TENDENCY TO BLAME OTHERS FOR OUR MISFORtune and to maintain grudges for a lifetime. To be truly free, we must forgive; we must forgive others and ourselves. Forgiveness does not equate to self-sacrifice or a release of our morals and values, nor does it imply weakness. On the contrary, forgiveness demands great courage and wisdom, for it necessitates evolution rather than conflict; it requires us to be above petty insecurity and stronger than anger.

- Life is too short and impermanent to lose friends, family, and companionship over the trivial inconsistencies of daily life and our need to be right.

In order to truly forgive, we must maintain a solid grasp on the meaning of our existence, on the manifest reality in which we live, and the true insignificance of our distorted perceptions of destiny and path. We spend a lifetime searching for connection; yet we are willing to lose that connection at the whim of our ego or faulty perception of reality. We find someone with whom we share a heartfelt connection; yet we allow our ego to take precedence over topics of little interest or impact.

- Our reality, relationships, and connections are based purely upon our perceptions.

In order to change the quality of our connection, we must change our perceptions. We cannot live in a constant state of judgment, nor can we live in constant fear of the terminality of our relationships. We can only live in this moment, the glorious present.

- The reality of forgiveness is simple in theory, but it is our own reality that stands in its way.

There is no right or wrong, no good or bad; there is only what is. Contrary to the ways and means of our society, we are not in this world to judge. We may not like everybody and we may not support everyone all the time, but we can accept them for who they are and find the beauty within them. We can love another, but that doesn't mean that we must like everything that they do. In order to fully accept another, we must fully accept ourselves, which is one of our greatest obstacles and opportunities in this life. Without forgiveness, we bring the strife and conflict of others into our day-to-day existence.

- Through judgment, we end up carrying the burdens of others instead of acknowledging and releasing our own.

We must forgive others—and ourselves—so that we can fully participate in the moment, experience full and total freedom, and appreciate the eternal beauty that exists within and around us. The only way to be fully present in this moment is to be fully present in this moment; there is nothing else of greater consequence.

- We must embrace the opportunity before us in this moment, as it truly is the only opportunity of any consequence—the only moment that has ever or will ever exist.

Acceptance

How can we be fully accepting of those we love?

How do we fully accept ourselves?

If we don't love ourselves, can we ever fully love another?

Acceptance & Unconditional Love

There is nothing noble in being superior to some other person.
The true nobility is in being superior to your previous self.
—Hindustani Proverb

- How can we accept another when we are restricted by our judgment of them?
- Can we truly love another when we cannot see their greatness beyond their faults?
- How do we fully accept another if we are unable to accept ourselves?

It may be said that intimate connection with another is the ultimate test of unconditional acceptance. So to speak, it is the appreciation of the magnificent rose along with a respectful acceptance of its stem of thorns.

- Full acceptance and unconditional acceptance require broad awareness.

Moments of deep love and emotional and intimate connection can bring us to alternate realities and feelings of momentary perfection. Seconds later, we may find ourselves amidst strife and introspection, forcing our love into a forgotten reality as we are overpowered by the darkness of our emotions. Though we may be embarrassed and confused in retrospect, we may launch a relentless campaign to be "right." Eventually, our heart overpowers our mind, and we make the sacrifices required by love, exploiting our most basic desires in the process. In an attempt to clear the air, we breathe and deeply connect to one another, exposing our vulnerability as we share and enlighten the shadow world within.

~ We feel and appreciate our commitment and connection, allowing our humility and humanity to seep through. It is then that we come to fully appreciate and accept the humanness of another.

Who would say a surgeon is more significant than a nurse or a school principal more vital than a teacher? Who would say that the supermarket cashier is more important than the bagger, the executive more central than the pipe fitter? We may compensate people differently, but that in no way is a direct reflection of their contribution. In nature, who is granted more credence — the spider or the snake, the lion or the horse? The choices we make move us toward the fulfillment of our deepest desires.

Nature's balance evolves through the integration of all facets of life. Are we dissimilar from the organisms that have acted as Earth's caretakers before us, maintaining it for billions of years? Or is it our human selfishness that invokes the destruction of the planet's resources? We all play a unique role in this game of life, a life in which we must consciously choose. The sooner we achieve personal acceptance, the sooner we may gift ourselves the truth of our path and destiny.

~ Our society is diseased by a past centered entirely upon educational conformity and a consequential restriction of the true independence of humankind.

We are taught to integrate into society, to follow a traditional order of events toward the greater good of humanity, yet this often results in the sacrifice of our inner truth for the perceived common good. We can fully embrace the evolution of humankind by teaching acceptance of the individual, by accepting others in their truth and greatness.

~ To fully love and accept another is quite possibly the most difficult challenge and greatest opportunity available to all of humankind.

The time has come to stop looking at one another as different or better or worse. We must stop comparing ourselves to each other by judging ourselves through our collection of assets and accomplishments. We can relinquish our judgment and accept our shared human existence however varied it may seem from one person's experience to the next. We are all challenged by the same core lessons, the same types of opportunities, and the same compounding fears. We are all grounded in the basic need to love ourselves and to be loved by those around us.

~ Often caught between materialism and misunderstanding, we have forgotten that our greatest gift in the world is to experience and express unconditional love.

The opportunity to fully appreciate the realities of our environment is likened to embracing the rose's stem of thorns, so as to share in the magnificence of the flower. Anything that stands in the way of love for ourselves or for another must be avoided; love is truly all there is.

Control & Adaptation

I believe that every right implies a responsibility;
every opportunity, an obligation;
every possession, a duty.
—John D. Rockefeller, Jr.

- Why are we unable to control others? Why do we try?
- Why do we have a hard time even controlling ourselves?
- Why do we try to control everything that we don't fully understand?

WE SURELY CANNOT CONTROL OUR WORLD, OUR ENVIRONment, or even those around us, especially those we love. We can only control ourselves, and even then only with much diligence. At some point, we must support and fully release those others and give them the space to exist fully in the space of love, happiness and peace. By chasing after them in an attempt to try and force them to see the light, we often become enablers rather than mentors.

- We can affect change, make contributions, and potentially impact the outcome, but we are unable to control the outcome or the response to our actions.

We cannot control our friends, family, customers, business professionals, other oppressed nations, or even the weather. We can offer our services to those in need and then we must accept what we cannot control. We attempt to act consistently with a positive attitude, to temper our emotions and passion, but those activities and emotions are not easy to maintain. Western medicine and American science are based on the concept of controlling that which we cannot and doing our best to predict what is outside our control.

- We try to extend life, control sickness, and predict or prevent natural disasters.

We attempt to control fate to the best of our ability, but in the end, resistance is futile. Our options are severely limited, for we must control what we can and accept what we cannot. In truth, we control very little. Yet as a society, we tend to complain and consistently blame others or our higher Spirit for the reality of the choices we make.

- Acceptance is an evolutionary trait and one most trying when faced with adversity and pain.

Imagine a society that takes responsibility for its actions and the resulting consequences. A society where people are of service beyond the pettiness of everyday living and where our communities and governments take responsibility for the realities they inflict. We can all do our part. Even small actions from seemingly random individuals consistently spread the greatest levels of positive change throughout our world.

Relationship with Ourselves

The outward man is the swinging door;
the inner man is the still hinge.
—Meister Eckhart

- Don't we love and respect ourselves?
- Do we love and appreciate ourselves enough?
- Why can't we care for ourselves in the same manner that we care for others?

WE CANNOT DEPEND ON OTHERS FOR WHAT WE REQUIRE FOR our own internal livelihood. We cannot live a life of expectation and unrealistic hope or we will forever be disappointed and empty handed. We must remember that our path is ours and ours alone to fulfill. There are times when we naturally look outside of ourselves for love, respect, and affection in the attempt to fill a void within ourselves. But in truth, nothing outside of ourselves can ever fix anything within ourselves. We may even find ourselves in situations where we relive aspects of our childhood, feeling unfulfilled in relationships or friendships. We may feel the need to be praised or to be affectionately caressed far beyond what we can ever actually receive.

~ We all have an innate need to be loved, but in the manners that love can be and is expressed, our individual requirements can never be met outside of ourselves.

As a function of the relationships between two people, these aspects are natural and common requirements for a healthy connection. However, when attempting to fill a void within ourselves, our perception of what we desire or require may be far beyond what we can ever receive, as the problem may be more internal regardless of our efforts to blame our external environment. We must overcome the reality-based limitations of our existence that require certain external variables be met in order to achieve particular desired feelings.

~ We must find peace and fulfillment, happiness, and love independently within ourselves.

We can change our external environment, but we must look within for the answers we seek. Our true needs can only be met by finding the miraculous connection to our own Higher Consciousness. Only then can we experience the abundant and effervescent outpouring of love throughout every moment, regardless of outside circumstance.

~ Above and beyond our connection to the power of the Universe is our connection to ourselves, to our truth, and to our purpose.

We must find eternal interdependence with our Higher Consciousness and inner selves so that we are not looking outside for what we require within. Nobody can fulfill any aspect of our being, whether our internal void or a feeling of deficiency. We must be full within ourselves. We must be fulfilled within our soul in order to create relationships and connections that are based in respect, trust, love, and the opportunity to give all to one another.

- Throughout this life and our evolutionary path, we have the opportunity to surpass all limitation, to expand beyond the petty requirements of a physical life and an unfulfilled reality.

We have the opportunity to work through the repercussions of our childhood, to feel fulfilled and present in every moment. But we must relinquish the reflections of our reality that do not support the creation and manifestation of greatness in every moment. Many of these transitions occur over the course of time, but they are all achievable in a single moment, in every moment. By finding our balance independently, we have the opportunity to give all of ourselves in fulfillment of our life purpose and in the greater goal of an evolved community and society founded in love.

- We can all share the gift of love, life, and passion with all of those around us through connection and service, but only by respecting ourselves first and foremost.

Comparative Significance

Too often we . . . enjoy the comfort of opinion
without the discomfort of thought.
—John F. Kennedy

- In this world, why do we believe that some people are more important than others? Are celebrities, athletes, politicians and the wealthy really more important?
- How is it possible that all innately perfect beings will inevitably create levels of hierarchy that value one race over another, one gender over another, or one life over another?

WHY DO WE CREATE AN EXPOSED OR HIDDEN PECKING ORDER within our society by which we value others differently than ourselves, looking up to some and down to others? We are not different from one another other than by the results reflected in our world, by the trail we blaze. Our inherent potential and creative powers being equal, our lives are not a reflection of what we have been given, but of who we are and who we choose to be.

- We are superior to nobody, inferior to no one.

There is no hierarchy in the structure of humankind. There is no hierarchical structure in God's design or with any of us in service or on our path. We are here on a moment-by-moment basis, giving, receiving and experiencing what is available to us. Many times we personalize the insecurities, fears, and otherwise outward projections of others, perceiving them to be our own. We try to stay open to the world around us, yet we open ourselves to everyone else's dysfunction. We attempt to walk as vessels in the mind and image of God, available and of service to those around us. Unfortunately, we tend to absorb petty strife and confusion, anger and frustration, and instead of focusing on our own path, we end up taking responsibility for everybody else's.

- We tend to lose sight of the fact that not only are we all created equal, we *are* equal.

We attempt to maintain our focus even throughout periods of bombardment. We will all go through times of tremendous difficulty, intensity, and discord, but we also encounter our own opportunities for growth.

There is a dualistic superiority-inferiority complex in our society where we place judgment on those who are perceived to have or to be less. We look up to celebrities, executives, doctors and athletes while at the same time looking down upon janitors, the mentally or physically disabled, and even our peers and neighbors. What right do we have to judge those around us? What makes us better than anyone else? Only our perceptions powered by our ego can provide the illusions of being more or less than anyone around us.

- Most importantly, we judge our existence as a comparative relationship, criticizing ourselves for not doing more or being more while at the same time looking down on others—all of which is a function of our own insecurities.

Sometimes we wish we were more, believing somehow that more equates to better. We always lose when comparing ourselves to another. No matter our perception of anyone within society, we are all on our own path, carrying our own burdens, following our own plan, and doing the very best we can. Not all of us are successful in our own minds or even in the minds of others, nor does being rich, powerful, or healthy equate with success. There is so much more to life than our outward expression of achievement. But even if we don't feel successful, that doesn't mean we are stuck. In any moment, we can change our position or our reflection of reality; all it takes is a choice, the right thought in the present moment, to alter our patterns and allow us to find the peace we require within.

~ The sooner we can accept ourselves and others for who we are—equals in mind, body and spirit—the sooner we will fully understand the communal goal of a society centered in peace, love, and happiness.

Gratitude

Why do we have a hard time expressing our gratitude?

How do we express our gratitude for the opportunities we are given?

Throughout life, we are often faced with tremendous challenges, such as bankruptcy, death, accidents, or illness. What does our way of overcoming these challenges say about who we are? How do we survive?

Do our outer experiences help us to find the strength within?

Damaging Desires

The finest thing in the world is knowing how to belong to oneself.
—Michel de Montaigne

- Why do we desire so much?
- Why do our desires far outweigh our gratitude?
- Can't we just be grateful for everything we have?

WE HAVE SO MUCH TO BE GRATEFUL FOR, YET DESIRE TENDS to overwhelm even the best of intentions. Desire is the foundation for our entire capitalistic economy and is the basis for war, anger, hatred, arguments, struggle and every single unconstructive trait of humankind. Desire is at the core of every human conflict. Desire is potentially the most damaging trait of humankind, and unfortunately, symptomatic and problematic of our society.

- Desire can also motivate us to change, to evolve, to take action.

In its most primal state, desire is related to a deficiency, the lack of something or someone. In its deepest state, desire is an emotive responsive, a reflection of our need to give and receive love. Some say there are only two emotions, love and fear, and every other emotion is only a derivative. Fear is a reaction to our thinking patterns, to a potential future, of an external experience or an internal association.

> ~ As our world operates in perfect equilibrium, love requires its polar opposite, even though we have little to gain from fear itself, and everything to gain from maintaining a state of love.

Desire is the basis for every heinous human act throughout the history of humankind including terrorism, war, genocide and torture. On an incredibly superficial level, desire requires us to buy things we don't need, conduct ourselves in a way we would otherwise not approve of, and treat people in a manner we intuitively or innately would disagree with. The foundation of every problem in our community is as simple and complex as the craving called desire and our relationship to it.

> ~ Our world is in harmony when we can operate from a state of gratitude for that which we have and for that to which we aspire.

Is it possible to change? Can we convert our deepest desires into enduring moments of appreciation and acceptance for what we do have? Altering something that seems as minor as desire can affect a dramatic and systematic transformation in the entire operation of our lives. We can change; we can evolve. And just like everything else, it begins on the inside, within each of us.

> ~ Collectively, our greatest opportunity is to adapt ourselves to the here and now, in gratitude for what we have, centered in love and compassion.

If we could express gratitude for everything we have rather than focusing on what we lack, we would live in humble awareness as opposed to petty aspiration. We need to find simple ways to transform desire into appreciation, to relegate our focus from outside to inside, from external problems to an internal modification of our thoughts, emotions, and desires. Can we change or positively affect our world? By focusing on changes within ourselves, we can see and express gratitude in and around our communities. We have the opportunity to make positive, incremental impacts benefiting our greater communities, our society, and the world as a whole.

~ What we truly desire cannot be obtained outside of ourselves.

Society of Consumption

Man is condemned to be free;
because once thrown into the world,
he is responsible for everything he does.
—Jean-Paul Sartre

- Why do we need to purchase things in order to feel better about ourselves?
- At what point does work become more important than family?
- When do we draw the line and realize that the fulfillment we require is only available from within?

OUR SOCIETY AND ENTIRE ECONOMY IS PREDICATED ON THE need to regularly purchase goods and services and extend the alleged and perceived reach, quality, and power of those purchases. We are all contributors, but how did we become so dependent upon this pattern of capitalism that we purchase goods and services we neither need nor truly desire? We inevitably perpetuate this system and, through example, train our children to desire the acquisition of "things."

- Blame the media, our community, or even corporations for helping to create excess demand for goods and services, but greed is not of their doing.

We are surrounded by empty desires, fruitless demands, and find it difficult to distance ourselves from the burdens that compel us to work more hours, lessening our quality time with the very family for whom we work. Perhaps we work extended hours in order to run from the dysfunction of our family dynamic. Perhaps it's our own life that presents the dysfunction we run from. Or perhaps it's the void from within ourselves that perpetuates the problem more than we can consciously accept or take responsibility for.

- We search outside ourselves for the fulfillment that can only be found within ourselves. And inevitably we choose hard work in lieu of fulfilling work, long hours instead of deep connection, and subsistence instead of happiness.

As a culture, we have much to be grateful for, and although as a society we are more prosperous than the majority of the global population, we are never short of complaint. Most of us have more than enough money to live joyful lives and provide for our families. But rather than choosing simplicity, we choose physical over spiritual abundance, a larger mortgage over our emotional well-being.

- We make decisions that force us to perpetually sacrifice. As a result, we not only provide less of ourselves to our loved ones, we become less as a result.

Many of us are driven to succeed for our ego, for our pride. And we find it eternally difficult to achieve balance and fulfillment when making decisions from the pettiness of our being. We can eliminate the choices that take us out of balance, allowing us to make decisions that enable our happiness and a quality of life we can share with those we love. We need a healthy balance between our requirements and our desires.

- We must be honest with ourselves as far as the sacrifices we make and what our livelihood truly requires in order for us to find true happiness and lasting fulfillment.

Our economies of endless demand do not promote humility. We are taught to focus on desire over necessity, opulence over gratitude. Our entire world is predicated on the basis of providing goods and services deemed *necessary*, however subjective that qualifier may seem. As our overt consumption breaches boundaries never before crossed, other communities are affected, altered in ways we have barely begun to consider or conceptualize. As our world does not have adequate resources necessary to continue our current rate of growth and consumption patterns, eventually we may not even have access to that which we physically require. We must be conscious of our desires, taking into account the balance and health of the planet as a whole.

- There is a distinction between incessant desire and living an abundant life. Desires control our existence; abundance is a side effect of a life well lived.

Prevailing Insignificance

We are happy when for everything inside us
there is a corresponding something outside us.
—W.B. Yeats

- Do we focus too much on the big picture while disregarding the moment?
- How can we obsess about the past and yet dream incessantly about the future?
- Why do we live in a manner that takes us out of the only moment that exists?

REGARDLESS OF THE BIG PICTURE, IT IS THE LITTLE THINGS that make all the difference. It is not the fancy cruise we took our wife on, but the flowers we gave her on the anniversary of her father's death. It is not the thousands of times we drove our daughter to school, but the time we took off from work to take her out for ice cream in the rain after she lost her big soccer game.

- We fail to recognize how much power we have over the current moment.

We can sit idly by and allow our emotions to control our experience, or we can take the initiative and change our thoughts, our feelings, and our reality in order to positively impact the few moments we consciously share with one another. We need to spend our time focusing on the power and experience of the moment, which we are so often prone to disregard.

- The problem is that life is made up of seemingly insignificant moments.

At the end of the day, we have to take responsibility for the reality we create. The experiences of our life are intentional; there are no accidents in the realities that we create. When put into perspective, life has the potential to be everything we desire: hopeful, happy, sad, peaceful, and brimming with clarity and kindness, openness and connectedness, even fear and hate. How quickly we forget that we are in the captain's seat, and all of the controls are at our fingertips. These few moments are all that we have, all that we share in what we call life.

- Each moment we have the opportunity to connect more fully, to share more meaningfully, to love more deeply, and to pause and truly appreciate every aspect of the lives we have chosen.

The little things in life are truly the biggest, the most meaningful. They hold the opportunity for true enlightenment if we can take our time and locate the magnificence within each and every seemingly insignificant moment.

The Gift of Parents

We love life, not because we are used to living
but because we are used to loving.
—Friedrich Nietzsche

- Why do many of us struggle with our connection to one or both of our parents?
- Why are we challenged to maintain the level of connection and intimacy we yearn for?
- Can we maintain gratitude and appreciation for our parents' existence and sacrifices, however minimal?
- Can we at least give them credit for our existence?

OUR PARENTS ARE THE REASON FOR OUR EXISTENCE. AND irrespective of the joy or pain incurred during our childhood, we can always find gratitude for the life they've given us that we now control. Often the lessons we learn as children are the foundation for the growth and contributions we make throughout our entire life. Some of us were born by what may have seemed to be an accident while others were consciously conceived. But at the end of the day, it was our parents who granted us the possibility of existence, and for that, even the lesser of parents deserve our appreciation. We must remember that irrespective of the experiences we incurred as children, our souls agreement was inclusive of the parents who brought us forth— there are no accidents.

> ~ No matter what pain and suffering we incur as children, our decision to live this moment in the potentiality of the future is the only one we have.

The intimate relationship is divinely guided as is the intimate act that brings a child into this world. When a baby is born, even "accidentally" in the mind of humankind, it is never an accident with respect to the Universe itself. We have the right to exercise choice, but all factors and opportunities of the moment are reflections of the past. All prior generations have sacrificed much, giving us the opportunity to live and experience everything this life has to offer. We often perceive their sacrifices, especially those of our parents, very differently than they do.

> ~ It is very natural to be in conflict with our parents, for we view them directly through the veil of the character and personality they have given us.

We can accept our truth for what it is, while expressing gratitude for the eclectic nature of the experiences before us which have brought us to this space of love, which we share with those around us. One day our parents will be gone, and we will have nobody to complain about and no one to forgive. We have only the time given to us. Beyond that, the world will outlive the footprints we leave behind. We must appreciate what we have been given as we reap the rewards of this life, which exist far beyond our comprehension.

> ~ Our childhood may not have turned out the way we might have hoped, but our parents deserve credit for the continued creation of life on this planet, namely you.

Remember that we are in control of our reality, of whom we choose to be, and of the actions we take. We give away our control by blaming our parents for the realities of our existence.

> ~ Blame is a poor excuse for not consciously choosing to live our magnificence.

We exert tremendous effort finding the perfect wife or husband. But we often don't realize that we marry our spouses' family as well and that we are subsequently connected to their extended family for the rest of our lives. The existence of our wife or husband and children is owed to these sometimes quirky, complex, and extraordinary in-laws. We never know who we are going to get as extended family when we fall in love. When a heart-felt connection with this new family is difficult to accomplish, we can still have gratitude and appreciation, for without them, we would not be blessed with the love of their offspring and the generations to follow.

> ~ Simply because we maintain gratitude for our parents doesn't mean that they will continue to be a positive contribution to our lives.

At times, we may be guided to separate ourselves from those we find harmful or disruptive to our life or to our contributions in this world. We may be guided to limit or even terminate our relationship with one or more of our parents as we move forward in life. It may be an important step to release aspects of our past that stand in the way of our greatness.

> ~ Nothing and no one can stand in the way of our path, our truth, or the purpose of our existence unless we allow it.

When Everything Is Great

We climb mountains because they are there,
and worship God because He is not.
—Mignon McLaughlin

- Why don't we ask for help when everything is going great?
- Why do we only ask for help when our lives are in turmoil?
- Do we get caught up in the pettiness of existence?

WE DON'T NEED HELP WHEN EVERYTHING IS GOING GREAT. When life is grand, money is flowing, and everyone is healthy, we are surrounded by love, and there seems to be nothing but joy in our lives. Why would we require assistance? When everything is a gift and we obtain everything we require, do we need to ask for more?

- We can only obtain happiness when we are grateful for what we have, what we desire equates to what we require, and what we have is what we need as we express our gratitude for everything in our life.

When the giving, flowing, or happiness stops or momentarily pauses—and it always does from time to time—petty thoughts and our perceived deficiencies see only the lack and absence in our life. In a moment of fear or scarcity, it can be difficult to recall previous moments of success, joy, or love. But inevitably they eventually return, for as we overcome that which stands before us, we realize that there is only love.

~ There is a reason for all things, and all things will pass.

When we get caught up in the lack, the pain, and the suffering, we are often paralyzed by its perceived power over our existence. We feel a true sense of helplessness, which does nothing to support our current situation, but merely feeds it the nutrients it requires to continue impacting and causing havoc in our lives. If we can find our center in these moments, to look beyond our lives and appreciate the opportunity for evolution and adaptation, expressing our gratitude for the opportunity to grow, we will more quickly overcome the challenges before us. Life itself is not complicated—it is in the details that life becomes love or is momentarily lost.

~ Life is a magical compilation of moments, a continually progressing chain of contiguous and semi-autonomous experiences.

It is in the moment, in this very moment, that we have the opportunity to obtain true peace, selfless love, heart-felt compassion, and intimate connection. In each moment, we have the opportunity to recreate these emotions with those around us. A future moment cannot bring us anything more than what is possible in this moment.

~ The moment in which you read this is the only moment that exists, the only one we are assured.

Every moment will not be pleasant, but it is our acceptance of *all* moments that allows us to evolve beyond survival, coping and continuance, to a life of joy and fulfillment, seeking the basic truths, the simple life, and eternal happiness. When we are able to find peace and joy within the moment, we can then utilize them to step back and appreciate the interconnectedness between all moments, which are understood only over the course of time.

We can study history to learn of conquests, terrors, magnificent moments, and peaceful outcomes. But we can only understand the reality of another time when we appreciate that history is only a compilation of present moments, which in the end formulate a pattern. This pattern, once accepted and subjected to the mindset of the many, becomes history. Our current moment is the history of tomorrow.

- The decisions we make today and throughout our lifetime are the future, which eventually become the past, and are used by our descendants to understand the pattern of our existence and to set the pace for the generations to follow.

Attitude

Is everything really possible?

Do we underestimate the power of kindness?

Why do we complain?

Why are we drawn to drama?

Attitude & Activity

What a man thinks of himself,
that it is which determines, or rather indicates his fate.
—Henry David Thoreau

- Why don't we believe that everything is possible?
- When we do believe that we can obtain what we desire, and what are we willing to give in return?
- Is life supposed to be easy?

OUR MANIFEST DESIRES CAN BE ACHIEVED THROUGH ACTION and attitude, through a focus on reality and mindset, through conscious and contiguous action. Aside from the tremendous influx of ancillary elements surrounding any desire, the presence of a good attitude, clear focus, inner joy, and intentional action provides for the creation of the results we desire. It is this clarity of focus and action, combined with our life path itself, that determines our outcome. Specific results are dependent upon the dreams and desires of the individual and what each of us is willing to give for what we desire.

- The universe works in perfect equilibrium, meaning that we must give in order to receive, whether consciously or subconsciously, and we cannot acquire or achieve what is outside the scope of our existence.

We cannot gain something without also being willing to give something of ourselves in return. In its simplest state, time and our related actions are choices we make in relationship to other less important opportunities available to us. For example, we cannot take time to do something for ourselves without taking time away from some other activity, from our family or from our work. As a result, through conscious and unconscious selection, we sacrifice one set of available experiences for another.

- In essence, in every moment we are making conscious decisions to engage in our reality, which emphasizes the required clarity and decisiveness necessary to manifest our desires.

In the same manner, we cannot fulfill our dreams without sacrificing some aspect of our physical, mental, emotional, or spiritual life. We can become wealthy, knowledgeable, healthy, or acquire the possessions we desire, but at the expense of simultaneous sacrifice. Without judging what we seek in exchange for what we surrender, our world stays in a perpetual state of inherent balance. We transcend reality to understand the significance of our desires and how they relate to the pre-destined path we follow. We may look at our lives and wonder how we ended up in our current situation, but the state of our lives is yesterday's outcome—the end result of our actions, attitudes, priorities, and choices that have led us here. Consequently, it is who we choose to be and the actions we choose to make that guide us out of one position and into the precise experience we have manifested for ourselves.

- As human beings, we have the tendency to struggle with a sense of entitlement.

Do we ever receive more than we deserve, or do we receive exactly what we desire and require? Finding the perfect balance of self-worth and intention allows us to appreciate every aspect of our lives while understanding that we can manifest anything that is available to us in this lifetime.

~ We must ask for what we desire because clarity and manifestation require focused thought and clear, decisive action.

Choose Positive

Diseases of the soul are
more dangerous and more numerous
than those of the body.
—Cicero

- Why do the media take such pride in dramatizing the negative aspects of our society?
- Why are we drawn to drama?
- Why does our society so frequently foster negativity?

SO MUCH OF OUR SOCIETY SEEMS TO REVOLVE AROUND NEGAtivity, as if the positive aspects of being human aren't as rewarding. Perhaps we relish the negativity of others as a welcome distraction from our own pain and suffering. Negativity is often used as if to present a flaw in the DNA of humankind, a warning sign that says, "Look, it's wrong, it's not perfect!" So what? Who said that everything was meant to flow painlessly and flawlessly from one moment to the next, from one person to the next, from one life to the next? The root of the problem is the dichotomy of our assumption of what is a perfect reality, when we believe that our current reality is filled imperfection.

- We move through life with the preconceived notion that we have an inherent right to perfection.

Our misguided belief is that a perfect world is one in which there is no hatred, bloodshed, or pain. We view our lives as compared to a dream, one in which everything is perfect, everyone is happy and fulfilled, without flaw or strife—"God's" vision. However, this couldn't be further from the truth, for life is based on growth, service, and evolution. The universe by its very nature is balanced and in equilibrium, regardless of our momentary perception of good versus bad, right versus wrong, or of being in or out of alignment. Life is perfect, for through its intricate balance, it is a reflection of all that exists in this world, all in perfect equilibrium.

- The acceptance and enjoyment of our external world is dependent entirely on the perfection we believe is within us and that which we perceive around us.

From one life to the next, we bring with us only the evolution of our soul as a function of the growth we have experienced throughout our existence. Our world is fraught with challenge and tremendous opportunity for growth and learning. The expectation of perfection is merely an illusion that leaves us empty and disappointed. We are here to do our part, to follow our path, and to live our truth in order to make this world a better place for ourselves, our families, our communities and future generations. We are here to do our best, to follow our path and our truth, and to impart all of the positivity of which we are capable.

- The rest is truly outside of our conscious creation and in the hands of our collective consciousness.

Wasteful Whining

I may not have gone where I intended to go,
but I think I have ended up where I intended to be.
—Douglas Adams

- Have we become a society of complaint?
- Why are we unable to take responsibility for our role within our world?
- Why is our lack of happiness the fault of everyone or everything around us?

WE ARE INDIVIDUALS OF INTEGRITY. WE MUST TRUST IN OUR path and our experiences without judgment, for our paths are divine in design. There is no sense complaining or whining about our path as our life is the sum total of every decision we have ever made. There is no one else to blame for either our experiences or our reality. That which we can control, we must take responsibility for. That which we cannot, we must merely accept. Through full acceptance of the life presented before us, we find no need to complain as we understand and respect that our life is exactly how it was meant to be.

~ Where we are headed is a reflection of where we have been, who we have chosen to be, and the choices we have made.

Nobody likes to spend time with people who find fault in all things because there is beauty in all things. When our eyes and our hearts are open to the magnificence of our world, the splendor overcomes the minutiae and the pettiness fades. We may waiver from time to time, but it is the strength of our resolve that allows us to see the splendid forest through the spindly trees. We make choices continuously, and the sooner we accept that we can only accomplish so much, the easier our lives become.

~ The Universe presents us with obstacles and lessons to the extent that we are able to handle them.

We have a tendency to blame others for every aspect of disappointment in our lives, as if all of the bad decisions made thus far in our life are everyone else's fault, not our own. By taking responsibility for our life, we take back the power of our existence and become fully responsible for our role in designing our life exactly how we desire. Everything outside of our control we must accept and release, allowing us to take responsibility for the lessons and the opportunities, the joy and the magnificence.

~ Remember, we can go anywhere from here . . .

Kindness Always

The best way to cheer yourself up is
to try to cheer somebody else up.
—Mark Twain

- Can we create the deep connections we require in life without kindness?
- Do we underestimate the power of kindness?
- Why is it so difficult to maintain gentleness, consideration and thoughtfulness?

KINDNESS IS ONE OF HUMANKIND'S MOST REMARKABLE QUALities, yet in our society, kindness is sorely undervalued. Kindness allows us to create happiness, joy, and peace from thin air, on a whim, and without a moment's notice. An act of kindness creates an air of peace similar to the way a smile can warm the heart, the sun can revitalize the body, and a loving embrace can calm the soul. We are in this world together, yet we often feel as though we are pitted against each other. Competition maintains the potential to advance technology and the evolution of our species, but it also can breed anger, hatred, and frustration. There are ways to achieve what we desire within our society that are true to our heart and soul. We can be thoughtful and respectful of all individuals, and we can stay on our path even while dedicating ourselves to creating a positive outcome.

> ~ It is not competition with one another that evolves our communities, but within ourselves to actualize our innate greatness.

Kindness is not always easy to offer. At times it requires us to look beyond our stress, exhaustion, and frustration to find our place of peace, understanding, and compassion. We may encounter others who may also be in search of truth, answers, peace, happiness, fulfillment and infinite wisdom. In this particular moment, they may be struggling to find their happiness and joy as they wonder how they are going to feed their family, pay their rent, or even stay engaged in this life. We don't have to change our vibration or become engulfed in their problems, but we can empathize and support. We can share our love and kindness to inspire and aid. We mentor others on the road to enlightenment by not sinking to their level, by giving them the opportunity to rise to ours, not from a place of superiority but from a place of joy, understanding, wisdom and peace. When our roles reverse, because they will, we can trust that those who love us will do the same.

> ~ The result of our contributions may be beyond our full understanding as our efforts reach beyond those we touch to people we may never meet. Kindness reverberates through eternity.

Community is about our connection to one another, and kindness is the primary method we use to engage and relate. Through interaction, we share or gift a part of ourselves, and in so doing, we allow an exchange of energy to take place. Contributions and philanthropy aren't only financial; giving exists beyond our physical contributions. Kindness is eternal, just as our character and our soul is perpetual.

- Life is too short to sacrifice the opportunity of the present to an ego-infested arrogance so common in humankind.

Kindness is not an action; it is a lifestyle. Gentleness and respect for others are not adjectives, but states of being. Our mind is the baseline of our reality, but it is also our private enterprise, available for public viewing only as a function of what we choose to share. The various methods in which we act and the choices we make define us as human beings within this world, but not of this world.

- We are not immune from, nor can we hide the truth of who we really are in our interactions with others.

We can strive to be more by giving more, letting go, and being less selfish and more caring toward others. Sometimes we appear to be egocentric hedonists. We make a difference by opening our eyes to opportunities to be of service. Through service we find true meaning, fulfillment, happiness, and joy. Kindness can heal and transform. Kindness has the power to deeply alter our communities.

- Through trust and kindness, we have the opportunity to deeply connect and to serve and share, consciously making the world a better place for all of us.

Mind Power

Do we have control over our mind?

Can we control what we think?

Can we control what we DON'T *think?*

If we cannot fully control our mind, and if our mind really is the basis for our reality, then is our reality outside of our control?

Power of Mind

Not being able to govern events, I govern myself,
and apply myself to them, if they will not apply themselves to me.
—Michel de Montaigne

- Does our mind have control over our world?
- How much control do we have over our mind?
- How do we fully embrace the power of our mind and its ability to impact our happiness and fulfillment?

FAITH HAS CONSIDERABLE SIGNIFICANCE IN OUR LIVES, AND not just because of its relationship to religion. Faith is our inherent belief or confidence in a person, concept or thing. It is our belief in the good nature of humanity. And it is our trust in a higher source, a higher purpose, and in our inner voice reminding us that anything is possible. In our soul and in our heart, we are always believers, which should be clearly distinguished from religion for the two are mutually exclusive. We trust and understand, for we are constantly connected to the greater power of Spirit itself.

- We are not seeking anything, for there is nothing to seek. All is here and now, in this precise moment.

We are spiritual beings having this physical experience, and it is our ability to successfully merge our physical and spiritual selves that creates the ultimate balance of life. We can reduce our current problems by allowing ourselves to be directly governed and guided by our heart and soul. Unfortunately, we have a tendency to allow the physical to direct our lives, with our entire experience controlled and filtered through our brain, our ego. Evolution requires an integration of our spirit with our decision-making, connecting our heart and soul, our subconscious and higher self.

- Our lives are run by our mind's decisions and perceptions, with strong guidance from deep within our soul, and through it all, our faith is continually tested.

The mind is far more powerful than we give it credit for. It has the power to control all sensory input and output, all processing, action, and all belief in order to protect itself and its role. The mind and the soul are often diametrically opposed. The soul looks to maintain its connection to source and the premise of a non-existent physical reality, while the mind looks to control and protect a corporeal reality where it thrives. Much as an alcoholic, a drug addict, or a schizophrenic is often unable to see anything beyond their reality, we as human beings are often unable see beyond the reality of our mind for the truth of our existence.

- It is our own attempted rationality of all things that endeavors to disprove that which we believe or innately know to be true.

Through science, religion, and society, we teach and support our children to trust what they are told. We tell them what to believe and what not to believe, who to trust and not to trust, and the structural elements of a life within this physical world. Children learn just as much from what we do as what we don't do, and less from what we say. Beyond what is taught, our children must reach beyond our societal teachings for their own faith and inner truth.

- True freedom is the re-discovery of everything that exists within this world based upon our own belief structure and vision for truth as directed by our higher self.

In order to see beyond our mind's influence, we are forced to trust our feelings from within, which often run contrary to what has been ingrained within us. As we begin to acknowledge those feelings, we must silence our mind in order to reveal the truth inside of ourselves. Nobody can tell us what to believe unless we inherently know it to be the truth, the gospel, or our inner knowing.

- All of the answers we seek are held deep within our soul, simply waiting for us to reach for them.

The World to Come

God has entrusted me with myself.
—Epictetus

- Why do we rule the earth? Was it merely our belief that created the fact?
- Are we really in charge, or is it just our perception of reality?
- Do we actually create our reality, or do we simply follow in the footsteps of those before us?

SCIENCE TELLS US THAT OUR UNIVERSE HAS EXISTED FOR BILlions of years, yet our personal incarnations number in the lowly hundreds of thousands. We proclaim a domineering control over our world, yet we pay the price of a future determined through the remnants of our petty obsession. We move slowly, evolve sluggishly, and progress unhurriedly as the fullness of reality seems beyond our comprehension. Unfortunately, our true powers seem restricted to the most advanced among us.

- Every one of us is the hope of an undetermined future.

Our lives are impacted by prior generations unable to fully experience their own communal evolution. We step into a pre-destined thought pattern, accepting possession and capitalism as a standard of living, professing our freethinking nature through scholarly stated opinion, and yet ignore our truth to become followers of our chosen leaders and complainers about the rest.

- Consciousness is so blasé, as responsibility and accountability scare the strongest of intention into hibernation.

We turn mock hopes and dreams into remorseless excuses for depression or classifications of our failure. We pay our debt of gratitude to those who have sacrificed before us by achieving more, obtaining more, and becoming more indebted to dysfunction—and yet our world gazes in envy and wonder at our "success." Congratulations, we have passed the test of time, becoming contributing citizens to a world created before our time and supporting and extending the foundation of greed for future generations. We follow an external reality that reflects the cold, shallow nature of a life without purpose, a pattern in which we have become accustomed.

- We have not consciously manifested this existence; we have simply stepped into it and allowed it to control our destiny.

The time for change and evolution is now. It is every moment. It is this moment. Our opportunities for growth are ever present, and we have full responsibility for the choices we make toward the fulfillment and transformation of our greater communities and ourselves. Evolution and greatness are side effects of commitment and truth, accountability and community, communication and purpose. Regardless of the situations or decisions that created our present moment, the future is ours, and we are the only ones who can change it.

- The time is now; the choice is ours.

Spiritual Union

The true genius shudders at incompleteness—
and usually prefers silence to saying
something which is not everything it should be.
—Edgar Allan Poe

- Is everything we perceive controlled by our mind?
- Are our feelings governed by our intellect?
- We can control what we say, but can we control what we sense, our feelings, or the energetic activity within our soul?

THE ACT OF SPEAKING IS A MENTAL ACTIVITY. THE ACT OF LISTENING is a mental activity. Everything that is communicated is processed in the brain, regardless of where it was initiated. It is impossible to speak or listen clearly from our heart or our soul in a verbal fashion as it is governed by the mind. The opportunity for soulful connection appears when we allow for the unfiltered love and joy of our heart to be expressed. Contrary to popular belief, in order to fully communicate with another, we need not necessarily verbalize. In order to really listen to another, it takes more than our ears.

- What is communicated or heard is rarely what was intended, no matter how consciously selected the phrases, no matter how clearly enunciated the words.

Communication is far more than the spoken word, just as spirituality is far more than going to services on Sunday. Communication is a sharing, merging, and commingling of energies, whether by gift, receipt, or overlap. As our energy fields intersect those with whom we connect physically, ethereally, or intentionally, many levels of communication occur. Sometimes we listen to a dear friend as they share with us a powerful and moving story of happiness or sadness, and while listening we become so engrossed that we cannot even hear the actual words they are speaking but become emotional as our tear ducts activate and our body pulsates as a result of the energy they emit.

- True connection cannot come from the mind, for it is incapable of a heartfelt or soulful connection.

It isn't about relationship in the form of connection, and it isn't about the actual words that are spoken. True bonding, a true spiritual union, is the sensation and energy that is shared between two people on the physical plane and through the vibrations that occur on all other planes. True connection exists beyond the brain, for it is the result of all aspects of our being that we are able to share with another. If we really want to connect and communicate and to be *heard* in the deepest sense of the word, we must live beyond the spoken word. It is as though we can sit quietly in the presence of another and soak in their gentle breeze of spirit.

- At that point, interaction supersedes societal communication entirely and becomes connection in its purest form.

External Reflections

It is a man's own mind, not his enemy or foe,
that lures him to evil ways.
—Buddha

- Why do we often feel helpless with regard to our world?
- Do we pretend to be someone we are not?
- Why don't we take responsibility for our perception of reality?
- Why does societal change seem so exclusive?

OUR EXTERNAL ENVIRONMENT IS GENERALLY A REFLECTION of our internal environment. We are simple beings, and the very reality in which we live is a manifestation of the reality we live without. Exhaustively it is said that our thoughts create our reality, but never is it more prevalent than in our physical and emotional reality. We move through life believing that it is the reality itself that is to blame, that it is our physical environment, our workplace, or even those poor less-evolved souls around us that are to blame for our inadequacies. We fault Spirit, the Universe, the sun, the dirt, the weather—anybody or anything other than ourselves—whatever will relinquish our responsibility. Why do we find it so difficult to take responsibility for the choices we make and the situations we find ourselves in?

> ~ There is no glory in a life when we only take responsibility for its positive aspects.

Not only must we take responsibility for the reality we manifest around us, but we must also respect the role of others as they affect the world in which we engage. Our world is merely a conglomeration of individual realities, a multiplex of sensation, reflections, and intentions that make up our communal externality. Societies that live through a reality so adverse, so contrary to the way of peace and love, become a society of strife, of suffering, and one that sorely requires our assistance.

> ~ When parts of our outer world demonstrate a life contrary to our inner wisdom and truth, we have the opportunity to set an example of what it means to stay true to our path.

We often feel so helpless. What perceptively little good we can provide seems to make little headway against the stark realities before us. Witnessing children suffering of hunger, the harsh realities of civil unrest, violent dictatorships, and even natural disasters, we find the idea of a world overseen by a God-like governing entity absolutely preposterous. However, we must remember that our world is in eternal balance and the pain and suffering we experience is only in relation to the opportunities we are given to grow, evolve and change. We cannot change regimes or our collective consciousness overnight.

> ~ We have the opportunity to follow our path and life purpose as part of our divine plan to contribute to a societal global evolution.

Perhaps we were not designed to recognize the correlation between our thoughts, perceptions, and reality. This would explain the difficulty in making the direct correlation and the challenge of injecting consciousness into every aspect of our lives. We take baby steps in understanding the true impact of our positive societal contributions. We are exactly where we need to be, and our society will eventually and collectively evolve as it needs to in order to appreciate the enhanced and eternal sensations of peace and love.

- Through positive and yet often perceptively miniscule contributions, our time will come, as will that of our greater communities, to evolve, and to appreciate the fulfillment and evolution of our collective consciousness.

Boundless with Opportunity

A pessimist is one who makes difficulties of his opportunities and an optimist is one who makes opportunities of his difficulties.
—Harry Truman

- Can we comprehend the opportunity of the present moment?
- Why does life require extraordinary and unimaginable humbleness and a powerful connection to source in order to feel complete?
- Where do time, life, and eternal hope exist as a function of our unconscious and infinite self?

LIFE IS SO MUCH MORE THAN THE REALITY WE SEE BEFORE US. It is the existence of our extended self that guides us and gives us the opportunities to grow, providing the space for our greatness. Our ability to grow and expand, to be present for transformation, is one of the most amazing gifts of this life. We may feel frustrated when working externally toward the goals we seek does not seem to bring them any closer.

- The time for existence unbounded by the pettiness of our physical life is here and available to every one of us for the choosing, for the taking, in this very moment.

Every day is boundless with opportunity, and yet we are often overwhelmed by our day-to-day tasks and responsibilities, preventing us from seeing the true opportunities before us. With one step, one breath, and one glance we can experience the reality of our choosing. One moment of eternal sensation or one glimpse of hope, and our life has thus progressed. Stillness, death, a rock, a mountain, we stop, we die, and life still progresses.

- No matter what the situation, the world moves forward with or without our conscious approval.

The continuation of life that we claim to be in control of is eternally self-sufficient and limitless. Time is the precarious evil of being, an excuse for the overwhelmed, overly abundant for the bored, yet existing in perfect equilibrium. The opportunity for balance within this obscure metric exists for every one of us, in our mind and in our world. We live our lives in the illusion of not having enough time, all the while attempting to stay present, to take advantage of opportunities as they are presented.

- We all wait for our turn to live, succeed, evolve, to find joy, and to eventually die as if there were a pecking order of existence.

As sure as the sun will rise, people will die, children will be born, and human existence will continue. We say to ourselves "now is the time" and "don't wait," but it appears that all we do is put off for tomorrow what we can do today. What are we afraid of? Why are we unable to move into the future? Are we afraid to change? Are we unwilling to let go of the illusion of the security and safety of the moment? Why are we willing to settle for less than we really are?

- We must move through the pain and growth of the opportunities before us, for they guide and assist us in becoming who we really are.

We must seize the opportunity to express outside the greatness within ourselves. Why are we never altogether ready to succeed in all areas of our lives, in every area of our existence? It is time to stop limiting ourselves, to utilize the guidance before us in order to fulfill our dreams, our aspirations, and our purpose within this lifetime. What are we waiting for?

- We are our own worst enemy. We are the ones standing in the way of our greatness. Get on with it!

Character

Why does it matter what anyone thinks?

Why can we control our character but not our reputation?

Does being human require certain incompetence?

Can we alter our perception of reality?

A Lifetime of Character

There is as much difference between us and ourselves
as between us and others.
—Michel de Montaigne

- Why does it require a lifetime to build a reputation but only a moment to destroy it?
- Why is our character a function of our life experience?
- Can we control our reputation?

OUR PERSONAL CHARACTER IS ONE OF THE FEW DISPOSItions entirely within our control. We are dependent upon the external world for reflection, but it is the manner in which we react and respond to what is presented that develops our character and conveys who we choose to be in any given moment. Our character is the integration and reflection of our integrity, honesty, self-worth, respect for ourselves and for others, and our ability to follow through on what we say. The core of character is our ability to follow our destiny and path of service throughout our lifetime. Character is not to be confused with reputation, for while our character is fully within our control, our reputation is not; it is controlled by the perceptions of others. Whenever we attempt to identify with an aspect of ourselves controlled by parties or elements outside of ourselves, we inevitably set ourselves up to fail.

> ~ We can only focus on who we choose to be in any given moment, which determines the quality of our existence.

Reputation is what happens outside ourselves; it is a reflection of those around us. Character is what happens inside ourselves; it is a reflection of our integrity and decision-making. Our character is representative of who we are and who we choose to be. Our reputation is a reflection of how society chooses to see and judge certain aspects of our being. We must release our attachment to our reputation given our inability to control it, for we can only focus our attention on that which we can control.

> ~ Our character is the outward expression of ourselves in this physical life.

We may spend a lifetime building character, but occasionally our actions run contrary to our truth. We have a tendency to live as a reflection of our past, in the shadow of our mistakes, but that does not create the space for our greatness. We have the ability to recreate ourselves in any moment, and we are not constrained in any way by our past or even our present.

> ~ The opportunities in life exist within this moment and are in direct correlation to our ability to listen to our truth.

Our full attention should be applied on the greatness of our being, our character. Every interaction is an opportunity to demonstrate the truth behind what we say and the heart behind how we act. In reality, the demonstration of our character is mainly rote response, unconscious and painless. When life throws us a curveball, we are forced to re-evaluate everything we have come to believe, accept, and understand,

and our lives become the ultimate test of our integrity. When life is most difficult, we often find ourselves conflicted in character, wanting to make the right decision, but discovering that the right answer is frequently the hardest one to follow.

~ The right answer is rarely the easy one.

If life were simple, we would never learn, grow, or have the opportunity to evolve or become our greatness. With free will, we do have the opportunity to choose the quality of our life, even one without passion and with no regard to our path or truth. Our character is a reflection of every lesson, challenge, and situation that pushes us, puts us over the edge, and tests our very limits. We are the sum-total of every experience in our life, the compilation of our history, of our choices, and the blending of time and space. Throughout life, we become the person we were destined to become only by taking advantage of the opportunities as they are presented.

~ Our character is a representation of who we choose to be in this and every succeeding moment.

Words are Meaningless

Trust only movement.
Life happens at the level of events, not of words.
—Alfred Adler

- Are we really kind and thoughtful? How intelligent are we really?
- Who are the greatest athletes of the moment?
- Why are our actions rarely in alignment with our words?

WE HAVE ALL HEARD IT SAID THAT *TALK IS CHEAP*, A REFLECTION of the ease and simplicity in speaking whatever is on our mind at any particular moment. We know that words and actions are very different things; too often we don't consciously select our words whereas our actions often require some aspect of intention. We easily pontificate about what we perceive as "just" or "right." We speak of many things and can even maintain the best of intentions, but our footprints are the true reflection of our path. Words spoken require only breath whereas action taken is more likely to be the reflection of our inner reality. We can speak easily of lofty ideals and inspirational messages, but it is the action behind the message that provides the truth of our being.

- The positive evolution of ourselves, our loved ones, and those in need requires resolve, commitment, and most importantly, action.

Who we are in life is a reflection of how we live within each and every moment, not merely the reverberations of our vocal cords. Politicians are the perfect example of career professionals who can speak gallantly, sharing words of wisdom, with actions that often speak otherwise. Why are our words not in alignment with our actions? Are our words disingenuous, or is it our actions?

- Our actions are exact representations of who we choose to be in any particular moment.

It is our words that we may distrust, for they rattle off our tongue as easily as the wind blows through the trees. Ask anyone who they think is the best basketball, football or baseball team, and you will receive a multitude of responses. In retrospect, these decisions are relatively easy when analyzing history, yet in truth any sports team is only as great as they are in this exact moment.

- We are only as evolved as we are in this exact moment.

You may say that you are a kind and thoughtful person, but you are only as kind and thoughtful as you are in this moment. You may proclaim that you are philanthropic, but only as a function of your giving in this exact moment. This moment is the only one that exists, for it is the sum total of your choices up to this moment, the exact reflection of who you choose to be. We see sports teams excel at various times, but it is the team that wins today that is the better team of the moment. Similar to life, it is our ability to be fully present in this moment that determines the truth of our existence, and who we are is who we choose to be in this moment and this moment alone.

- We cannot live off past success just as we cannot accumulate sleep nor live off the food we digested years ago.

Many of us move through life proudly proclaiming to be a certain type of person, whether spiritually, emotionally, physically or otherwise. We proclaim our efforts to be of service, to give, to succeed, and to share our kindness. However, our words carry little weight in comparison to the actions that take place beyond them—not yesterday, but today. We are only as loving as we are in this moment. We are only as forgiving as we are in this moment. We are only as respectful as we are in this moment. Our moments can fall apart and temporarily degrade into our weakness, but it is who we are in this particular moment that is the truth of who we are. At any moment, we are the perfect and direct manifestation of our being.

- Decide carefully, for in this moment you are the person you choose to be.

Downfall of Competence

Learning without thought is labor lost;
thought without learning is perilous.
—Confucius

- Are we all incompetent?
- Are we able to increase the quantity and quality of our work at the same time?
- Do we expect more while at the same time wanting to do or give less?
- Are we the center of our universe?

AS A SOCIETY, WE ARE SO FOCUSED ON MULTI-TASKING AND accomplishing more with the limited time available that we rarely enlist enough focused energy or patience to complete any activity appropriately. We drive haphazardly, throwing caution to the wind as we endeavor to multi-task in every area of our lives. We listen to the news, catch up on phone calls, read emails, send text messages, and drink our coffee—all while driving to work. We have conversations with our peers, friends, or families while we work on the computer, and wash the dishes. Instead of listening, we think about what we are going to say next.

- Our lack of focus as a society is symptomatic of the current condition of our world.

We do more in quantity with less quality. We expect more but want to give less or pay less. We want to work less but make more money. We want to live in bigger, more luxurious homes, purchase fancy cars, compile luxuries, and still have time to appreciate and take advantage of them all. We are conflicted in our society, individually and collectively, as we attempt to fulfill our life purpose yet spend the majority of our days walking the lines of societal confluence, regaling in the shallow fulfillment of our hedonistic accomplishments.

- We look everywhere for the fulfillment we desire, and as a variable of our overly competitive society, we find ourselves trying to outdo each other for the petty physical comforts we create for ourselves.

This viscous cycle provides little progress toward the internal peace and prosperity we desire. The external world is a reflection of the internal, and we need merely look within for what we are without. When our world is in strife and our reality is in conflict, we need to look within for the evolution and fulfillment we inherently desire. We must find our own clarity of purpose. We must focus on what is most important, above and beyond that deemed so by societal standards. It is not the length of our lives that is important, but the quality and impact we are able to exert during our lives.

- It is the quality of our work, our relationships, our communication, and our life efforts that determine the quality of our existence.

Manifest Reality

I simply believe that some part of the human Self or Soul is not subject to the laws of space and time.
—Carl Jung

- Why is it so hard to alter our perception of reality?
- Why are psychics or healers only able to observe certain things?
- How do we alter our belief structure or change our beliefs?

THE WORLD AND EVERYTHING IN IT IS PURELY ENERGY. LOOKing into the energy field of an individual, a talented psychic or reader will be able to see the past, present, and future as a reflection of the present. However, whatever can be seen will only manifest as a result of decisions on the part of the individual. No matter what can be read and determined, we are beings of free choice. The path of predetermination is limited only by destiny, which becomes a reality only as a result of the conscious decisions we make in every moment. By changing our understanding of the moment, we directly change our perceptions of reality in the moment and the ones to come.

~ All experiences are interrelated, yet we have the power to change.

The world as it appears to us in any given instant is merely a reflection of our experiences and understanding consolidated into this present moment in time, but can be better understood as a direct reflection of the past. We need not alter our experience or environment in order to obtain the evolution and advanced understanding we seek. By altering our perception, our belief structure, a chain reaction occurs almost instantaneously that adapts our reality, our world to a new level of understanding.

~ All things being equal, our environment is merely a reflection of the "invironment," or prior internal processes as reflected externally.

Belief structure is the basis for our thoughts and actions, and to change our world we must alter our belief structure. Our belief structure may be ingrained from childhood or even from prior lifetimes. Altering our belief structure can be more complicated than it seems and may require assistance from those trained in various healing modalities. We begin by becoming aware of and eventually removing the emotional or spiritual blockages that stand in the way of our happiness and fulfillment. We become dependent upon others within our community to help us along our way, to assist us in clearing and releasing what is necessary. We can work together to obtain the guidance we require.

~ We can evolve to the point where our thoughts manifest instantly as our reality and our world becomes consistent with our desires.

Heart

Where can we find our truth?

How do we create true heart connections?

Why don't we ask for help?

Why do we look outside of ourselves for our own evolution?

Follow Your Heart

You'll never find peace of mind until you listen to your heart.
—George Michael

- Where do we find the answers?
- Who and where do we go when it seems that we are backed into a corner with nowhere to turn?
- Where can we look to be guaranteed the truth?

We are all in search of the truth, the guide map, directions, the handbook, or Holy Grail for the answers to our own personal life and earthbound reality. Many of us fail to realize that the answers are presented to us in obvious form, accessible to those open to a life of guidance; receiving the answers is a function of the inherent simplicity in our lives. When in doubt, it is our connection to a higher power, to our higher selves, that provides the answers and guide maps to the evolving destinations we seek.

- At times, the path of least resistance is the one we are attracted to, but the easiest path isn't always the right one.

We are often guided to choose the difficult path in life, even when following these paths results in the ultimate tests of our commitment, resolve, and integrity. The Universe pushes us to our limit, and in the most difficult of situations, it is our dedication, integrity, and resolve that is tested. When we reach our limit and feel we cannot handle any more, we are often presented with even greater opportunities for growth. We soon discover that we can handle more than we ever imagined. It is within this reality that we live or die, succeed or fail. It is within this reality that we allow ourselves to suffer or ask for guidance and assistance as we begin to understand our continual opportunities for fulfillment and evolution.

> ~ At times we face extreme challenge and pain, but the path is clear when we choose to see it.

We need to eliminate the misnomer that our path is designed to be easy—but we can make the best of the opportunities we are presented. We cannot make comparisons or judgments of our current path as it compares to that of those around us, for each of us is presented with experiences specifically designed for our own learning and evolution. Each of us will experience diverse hardships at different moments in our lives in entirely different ways, yet we all face our own path with the prospect of overcoming whatever obstacles we face.

> ~ Each of us will face and, hopefully, conquer our own inner demons; it is only the color of our pain that deviates from one soul to another.

As human beings, it is our duty to fully experience this life, whether through physical pain or the complete dynamics of human emotion. We are here to fully experience what is presented, but we must be careful not to identify ourselves with what we feel. We may experience pain, but we are not our pain. We can feel for but mustn't identify with the feelings that are not true to our core, not consistent with who we know ourselves to be. We are often blind to the most obvious realities of our lives; through sight we gain consciousness, and with realization we obtain the clarity and strength to embrace and overcome.

- By choosing not to see what stands before us, we choose ignorance over evolution.

Our world is controlled by our mind, and it has a habit of playing tricks on us as it attempts to conform to the status quo, convincing us that change is hard and unnecessary. However, through our truth and inner knowing, we must regulate our mind so that it recuses itself as we obtain the guidance we require, setting ourselves up for greatness. Evolution is consciously achieved by those of us who choose to see what is presented, who face the realities of our existence head-on.

- We have the opportunity to evolve and find fulfillment by making the often difficult but correct choice, even in the face of adversity.

Intimacy in Relationship

Shared joy is a double joy; shared sorrow is half a sorrow.
—Swedish Proverb

- Why do we try to handle everything on our own? Why don't we like to ask for help?
- Why is maintaining heartfelt connection the hardest when life is most challenging?
- Is it possible to experience intimacy in every relationship, outside of the physical connection with which it is generally associated?

WE COME TO THIS WORLD TOGETHER; OUR SURVIVAL depends on our level of interconnectedness. From time to time, we all need the assistance and love of those who care for us, of those whom we love. There is no profession that can be undertaken alone, nor can genuine service be accomplished without the existence of someone or something to serve. Our success in life is fully dependent upon the reception of those we serve and those who serve us. We are blessed with guardians and guidance around every corner when we open our eyes, hearts, and souls. We can then open our mouths and express the sanctity of our world, learning to articulate and connect through service.

⁓ We must seek intimacy in all relationships, connecting on a level where our hearts open and our souls peak outside of ourselves and we share the ultimate of human emotion.

This is not necessarily physical intimacy; for that level of expression is one that can operate from a wide range of vibrational levels. We have the opportunity to experience intimacy in every relationship and in every connection, simply by living our truth and expressing ourselves from the highest vibration possible. Intimacy is often demanding and challenging because it requires us to let down our defenses while increasing our risk of being hurt. Many times, it is those we love the most with whom we also have the most heated conversations, the greatest struggles, and the most significant emotional triumph. It is the intensity of love that fuels the depth of our emotions. Love and hate are not dissimilar; they are polar opposites but innately intertwined. It requires the same level of emotion and passion to fuel love as it does to fuel hate. Many times what we hate is the very foundation for what we love and vice versa.

⁓ Divorce has a tendency to be so incredibly heated and emotive, as the emotions used to destroy a relationship are a reflection of the ones used to create it.

We have the opportunity to choose our reaction and emotion in every moment. Just as we can choose to hate, alternatively in the same moment we can choose love and thus transform our entire reality, instantly impacting our sense of peace, wellbeing, our perceptions, and the associated choices we make.

⁓ Conscious selection of our actions and reactions is a direct result of who we choose to be in any given moment.

Given the limited resources we have available to commit to this lifetime, why would we sacrifice our energy in a manner contrary to our natural evolution? By focusing on our greatness instead of our pettiness and by appreciating and sharing love rather than hate, we have the opportunity in every moment to be in the fullness of ourselves, to live our truth. We may choose to change our external environment as it becomes uncomfortable, but every discomfort serves a very particular purpose.

> ~ We must remember that we can change any relationship, but if an opportunity for growth is presented and ignored, it will follow us in perpetuity until we resolve it.

When challenged or confronted with an opportunity to grow and evolve, in every committed relationship we inevitably find ourselves at a crossroads where the effortless choice is to change the scenery, to walk a different path, or to go in the opposite direction. However, evolution occurs by directly and consciously facing our reality and making choices in alignment with our truth—choices that positively contribute to our world, irrespective of the dynamic in which we find ourselves. When life gets difficult, that is our precise opportunity to reconnect, to open our heart, and to listen to our truth. We cannot receive fulfillment from those around us or from anything outside of ourselves. Through connection, through the sharing of love and intimacy, we reconnect with the truth within ourselves.

> ~ We are all given the tools and the opportunity for eternal fulfillment in all areas of our existence; we need only open our minds, hearts, and souls to find what we seek.

Heartfelt Connection

Once a word has been allowed to escape,
it cannot be recalled.
—Horace

- Why is it so hard to find true heart connections?
- Why are we inclined to speak poorly of others?
- Is the weakness we see in others a reflection of what we see within ourselves?
- Why do we look outside ourselves for our own evolution?

OUR WORDS ARE VIBRATIONS THAT TRAVEL IN PERPETUITY, not just to those within earshot, but to the universe at large. Anything we say in private is stored in perpetuity. Sooner or later, the truth of our being is exposed for all to see, which is reason enough to find the goodness within and stay true to our purpose and path. When speaking from our hearts, regardless of to whom we speak, there is always something magnificent to appreciate and adore. As spiritual human beings, we need not like everyone for who they choose to be in any given moment, for what they do or have done, or even what they believe in—but we can love them just the same.

> ~ The beauty of sharing the magnificence of another is a priceless endowment that changes lives and has the potential to change our world—even if only for one moment and one soul at a time.

We can avoid petty negativity and drama merely by seeking out the very best, the absolute positive, in all people and in every experience. We are all spiritual beings walking the path of evolution with the potential for momentary enlightenment, yet with the same strife and tribulation afforded to all on our path to greatness. We can appreciate the beauty of everyone around us, and in so doing find a deeper appreciation not only of ourselves, but of the global interconnectedness of all beings. We can love and appreciate everyone around us, not because of their actions or even their belief systems, but simply because of who they are.

> ~ We can always find magnificence when we open our eyes and our hearts.

By focusing on the negative, we merely project outwardly the insufficiency within ourselves, focusing on the aspects of ourselves that are contrary to our truth. In order to fully understand the pain of another, we must come to grips with the pain within ourselves. We are all beings of positive and negative, yin and yang, black and white, light and dark, but it is on our path that we are able to leverage the balance within ourselves to create peace in our life. The heartfelt connection we maintain within ourselves and that we desire from others is what we are here to share. Through conscious awareness, we are able to focus on the positive, in essence sharing what we desire for our own life and creating our world in like form and fashion.

> ~ We can walk the path of integrity and sincerity, but it requires action as much as it requires thought, for a life of evolution and magnificence is available to every one of us, but we must choose it and we must act on it.

Friendships

Do friendships have a purpose?

Why do we struggle with commitment?

How do we create deep and fulfilling friendships?

Do some friendships naturally whither?

Nurturing Relationship

Let us be grateful to people who make us happy;
they are the charming gardeners who make our souls blossom.
—Marcel Proust

- Do we nurture our relationships?
- Can we control our relationships?
- Do we ever evolve beyond the other party to a relationship?
- Can relationships ever be in perfect equilibrium?

WE HAVE RELATIONSHIPS WITH OUR CHILDREN, OUR FRIENDS, our family, our peers—and of course our most important relationship with Spirit, God, or ourselves. Within these relationships we cycle through various stages of learning, growth, and understanding. The relationship itself becomes a living and breathing organism with needs, expectations, and desires of its own. We nurture the relationship with ourselves and with those we love, similar to how we nurture our children. Just as our lives are a succession of lessons and growth, so are the relationships in which we participate and co-create. Our relationships move through their own stages of development and through extensive learning and growth. Relationships evolve just as we do, generally in a non-linear fashion.

> ~ The longevity of a relationship is predicated on the continued nurturing and inherent necessity of the relationship itself.

A relationship by its very definition requires the involvement of multiple parties. Healthy relationships require a commitment to ongoing growth and evolution. However, at some point in a relationship, there is often one party who evolves beyond the other, causing the dynamics of the relationship to change. A relationship of peers eventually becomes one of mentor or mentee. A relationship of parent to child eventually reverses as the child is required to care for the parent. Either the under-evolved party in the relationship will grow and evolve to a point of shared understanding and a common vibration or there will be disharmony, and the relationship may suffer. The being of a relationship becomes an entity that maintains the needs and requirements of each party, and it is through this connecting of souls that we can evolve and grow together. The various roles we play continually adapt and change, resulting in a living and breathing organism, a dynamic of growth and opportunity.

> ~ We control what we can, and we release what we cannot.

We have full control over ourselves, and we have absolutely no control over anyone else. So a relationship is a true anomaly in that it is controlled by both parties; however, not necessarily equally. As it requires two people to create a relationship, it only requires one to terminate it. An oak tree can grow for hundreds of years, overcoming the most commanding storms, droughts, and environmental displeasures, yet in one destructive moment, it can be eliminated forever. It requires two people to heal and support a relationship, but it merely compels one to destroy it. As with any being, existence of relationship is predicated upon need.

~ Once the need has been absolved, the being or entity of relationship will either transition or dissolve.

The Third Being

He felt now that he was not simply close to her,
but that he did not know where he ended and she began.
—Leo Tolstoy

- Beyond each party to a relationship, does the relationship itself have a path, a destiny, a purpose?
- What is the energy of a relationship, and how do we nurture it?
- How do we support the natural evolution of our relationships?

WHILE WE NATURALLY ASSUME THAT OUR ONE-TO-ONE RELATIONSHIPS are made up of ourselves and the other party, there is a third entity that is the actual energy or being of the relationship. It is in this entity where our relationship truly exists, beyond the autonomous operation of ourselves individually. Just as we each are energy of a certain vibration, our connection is also energy, an ebb and flow, a heartbeat with a purpose and a destiny. Relationships maintain intention, trust, purpose, and a lifeline all to themselves. This third "being" must be maintained, nurtured, and supported by both parties in order for it to operate and survive as a healthy, evolving organism.

- In relationship, we tend to focus first and foremost on our own needs and desires, and we look to the other participant for fulfillment, love and to obtain what we desire.

When in crisis, we have a tendency to blame the other party to the relationship rather than taking responsibility for our role in the situation in which we find ourselves. Beyond projection, blame and "extrospection," we eventually learn to look inside ourselves for understanding, meaning, and truth. There is nothing we truly desire that can be fulfilled outside of ourselves. We must go inside to understand our role within any situation, crisis, or misunderstanding.

- Our happiness, evolution, and fulfillment are ours alone, and nobody in this universe has control over the most important facets of our existence.

As we invest in obtaining what we desire, we develop the clarity to know what we want and don't want. In romantic relationships, we invest our resources, our time, and energy, whether through seeking, manifesting, or happenstance. Once we jointly create a relationship, we are conjoined into a shared third entity, that "being" of relationship itself that we mutually impact and control. Over time in an intimate relationship, we have a tendency to retreat to some of our independent ways, taking our partners or spouses for granted and forgetting our destiny with this third being. We may eventually focus or blame the other half of the relationship with judgment, resentment, and projection.

- Our opportunity is to evolve to the point where we look only to ourselves for the answers and for our truth.

In order to understand the world outside ourselves, we must first look deep within to ensure that we are coming from a high place of peace, independence, and clarity. In so doing, we free the other party in our relationship from our judgment or blame and re-open the space for connection and love. When we retreat inside to heal, rebound, and recover, we may discover that it is the third entity of the relationship that requires our attention for its own healing and rejuvenation.

- Relationships do end, and it might be that we have just grown apart—in the sense that we have evolved at a different rate, and healthy relationships require that we operate on the same vibration.

When, for whatever reason, we stop investing in the relationship itself, we have a tendency to blame each other or ourselves. We must remember that the birth of a relationship is similar to the nurturing of a child and requires patience, sustenance, and even freedom, trust, and respect. Our relationships will change and evolve, sometimes even to what may feel to be our detriment. In order to maintain a healthy relationship, a commitment is required from all parties to invest time and energy in the support of the relationship itself.

- We make a commitment to the vision of the relationship, to its future, and to its health and happiness.

We make a commitment to the continual evolution of our relationship, and when it is gone, we mourn its loss as if something extremely important has been taken from us, and in some sense, it has. When our relationships end, we must fight the tendency to retreat to our lower vibrations. We may be inclined to think that love is lost and unattainable, but we must trust and have faith in the magnificence and potentiality of this existence.

- When the time comes, we must be willing to let go and move forward in life, for when we release our partner, we also free ourselves.

Good Friendships

Wherever you go, go with all your heart.
—Confucius

- Why is it so hard to make deep, long-term, connected relationships?
- Are we so complex, so difficult to be around that finding solid companionship is unattainable?
- Are we so unique that finding commonalities with strangers is problematic?

OUTSIDE OF FAMILY, FRIENDSHIPS ARE THE CONTENT AND lifeblood of this existence. Good friends help us stay on track and out of trouble, and they can assist us in maintaining our positive outlook, making the right decisions, and helping us fully enjoy and appreciate this life. We try to surround ourselves with like-minded people, those with similar beliefs, values, and attitudes; but it can be challenging. Some of our relationships can feel superfluous, especially when we aren't on the same vibration, when we don't share the same beliefs and perspectives,. We have associations on the surface, but inside we struggle to find the soul connections, the deep emotional relationships we long for. Sometimes we evolve faster than those around us, causing disharmony, and pushing us to move on and into the unchartered territory of the future.

~ There is an opportunity for learning and growth in every connection, in every moment.

With every momentary or long-term connection we share, we have the opportunity to see another's greatness, to see beyond the trite perceptions of the moment to something even deeper. In the same breath, we have the opportunity to give something of ourselves to even the most haphazard acquaintances and random strangers whose paths we cross. However, the deep connections we require are often more than what can be fostered in the perceptively random crossing of paths in this existence.

~ We must locate the souls who are here to assist us with our journey, and we must take the time to connect with our heart and soul.

We seek those who are going to help us raise our game, grow, and better understand ourselves as we deepen our reflection, while also allowing us to serve the relationship. In so doing, we create a connection with the potential to last a lifetime. Finding true companionship is one of the challenges and hurdles of this life. True fulfillment is found on the inside but can only be fully realized with the help of our connected brethren. Every day is an opportunity to locate and connect with those family members of another time. Much like improving or even mastering a sport or hobby, it requires effort, focus, and attention. Good friendships foster our ability to open our heart and soul, to assist each other and to collectively evolve.

~ In life, we must stand up for our greatness and attract those with whom we can connect on the deepest level while fostering our mutual evolution and fulfillment.

Intimacy

How important is intimacy to fulfillment?

Do we have a problem with commitment?

Can we fall OUT *of love?*

Is there perfection in relationship?

Can we fully accept those we love?

Intimate Connection

A friend is a person with whom I may be sincere.
Before him I may think aloud.
I am arrived at last in the presence of a man so real and equal,
that I may drop even those undermost garments of
dissimulation, courtesy, and second thought,
which men never put off,
and may deal with him with the simplicity and wholeness
with which one chemical atom meets another.
—Ralph Waldo Emerson

- Can we survive without connection?
- Can we thrive and find happiness without fulfillment?
- How do we foster connection and fulfillment as a natural course of our existence?

JUST AS WE CANNOT DRINK ONLY WATER TO SURVIVE, WE CANnot subsist without connection and fulfillment. Connection is not limited to our relations to others, but also to ourselves, to our soul, and to the Universe. We are complex organisms and need to be treated as such. Fulfillment requires connection of the soul beyond the superficial. We cannot fulfill ourselves through trite interaction, for it must be heartfelt, with a consciousness that offers those around us the opportunity to connect deeply to us.

~ We expose our vulnerability and "nakedness" as we share who we really are with each other, and through that sharing, we grow and evolve individually and collectively.

The superficiality that is often fostered within our society is one that breeds a certain distance that offers a safety net, allowing us to protect that which is most intimate within ourselves. Brutal honesty requires us to be naked to ourselves, to our world, to our communities, and to our loved ones. Exposing ourselves for our truth gives others the opportunity to love us for who we really are and not the protected projection of societal perfection that we strive for outside of our true selves. Honesty with ourselves and with others provides the guidance we require to stay on our path and to be of service.

~ We cannot follow a path of truth and purpose while pretending to be someone we are not.

Through a commitment to honesty, we can walk a path of integrity while eliciting the same level of respect from others. The only way to deepen our connection with others and surpass superficiality is through honesty and truth. Speaking and being our truth in all that we do is not to be confused with vocalizing everything that comes to mind; often the pettiness of the neutral mind is not the voice of our greatness but of mediocrity. We can have a conversation with others from our brain, but true connection comes from the heart and is only found by opening the very epicenter of our being with the truth that exists within us. We must share our emotions, our feelings, and our truth so that we create meaningful connections, relationships that are destined for greatness, and a support network of spiritual beings of purpose.

~ We must work together to manifest the greatness we not only demand of ourselves but of our greater communities and world at large, as well.

Committing to Greatness

A man without a wife is like a vase without flowers.
—African Proverb

- What exactly is marriage? Why has its significance been diluted over time?
- Beyond the legal bond, does marriage have any sanctity anymore? Is it a reflection of spiritual connection?
- Why can commitment be so difficult? Is it the fear of failure, or the fear of making an irreparable mistake?

MARRIAGE IS A UNIQUE ELEMENT OF AN INTIMATE RELAtionship, a level of commitment many of us balk at in every other area of our lives. We make a good-faith yet interminable commitment to our partner, and in order for it to succeed, we are often forced to release our ego, disregard our pride, and live for the betterment of ourselves, our partner, and the relationship itself. We commit to taking care of our partner until "death do us part." But why are we unable or unwilling to make the same commitment to our career, our employer, our spirituality, or most importantly—to ourselves? Why must we live a disparate connection to Spirit so that we ask for help only when we struggle? When life is great, we somehow nestle our connection to Spirit deep within our pocket.

~ We cannot be dualistic in our intimate relationship nor in any other relationship.

Over time, marriage has become less of a commitment and more of a convenience, a temporary arrangement with permanent repercussions. We quickly dismiss the nightmare divorce inflicts on our children, family, friends, our financial situation, and the important devastation we transgress personally. Rampant divorce is a symptom of a society in disrepair. People might divorce for a wide range of reasons. Perhaps they gave up. Perhaps one party grew and evolved beyond the other and realized that happiness is predicated on a greater level of fulfillment. Or perhaps relationships have a distinct timeline, a natural beginning and ending.

~ Seldom is hatred as strong as when it is the result of two people who previously loved each other.

In a fully open and committed relationship, we expose the greatness and darkness of our soul to our partner; we share aspects of our being that we rarely even acknowledge within ourselves. In deeply committed and intimate relationships, we open our hearts to levels that we are often unable to reach on our own. Beyond a life of love and companionship, there are times when we must part ways, but the pain, suffering, and anguish are reflections of the extent to which we loved.

~ There are times when we desire more, and if it cannot be obtained or achieved in our current situation, we must be willing to let go toward the possibility of what awaits us.

Given the commonality of divorce, most don't think of marriage as a lifetime commitment but merely a commitment of the moment. In a life dedicated to growth, where the moment is all we have, a lifetime commitment is entirely contrary to our belief system. In reality, we cannot actually make a commitment for a lifetime, for we don't know what the future will bring.

- The only commitment made with integrity is a commitment to the moment and to the love and happiness we share in that moment.

Fear of commitment is the fear of making a mistake, as if life's choices were irreparable. Perfection is futile and results in frustration, upset, and a destruction of self-esteem and personal good will. Life just isn't that serious, especially when we choose not to make it so. We cannot fail in life; that isn't how it works. We must merely show up whenever and however possible; growth and evolution are the inevitable side effects. We can make choices for the betterment of others and ourselves, but in the end, we will follow our predestined path and end up exactly where we need to be—as reflections of perfection.

- It is our commitment to the moment, to every moment, that provides the opportunity for greatness, evolution, and growth.

Spiritual Connection & Relationship

We must be our own before we can be another's.
—Ralph Waldo Emerson

- Is it difficult to find love in relationship?
- Is it as easy to fall *out* of love as it is to fall *in* love?
- Why are we impatient when searching for our soulmate? Yet when we do fall in love, why we are often unwilling to allow the natural evolution of the relationship?
- Why is it difficult to understand the ongoing evolution of each member of an intimate relationship?

LOVE IN A ROMANTIC RELATIONSHIP IS A FASCINATING dynamic, requiring the merging of energy on all levels. We fall in love as our bodies, minds, hearts and souls begin to merge; and as we fall, we invest in this newly shared foundation with the goal of eternity, or at the very least, longevity. When we find true happiness and joy, why would we ever want it to end? The foundation of such a connection is what bridges the gap when personal evolution demands adaptation.

Irrespective of our current joy, the man or woman whom we love now will not be the same person we love 10, 20 or 30 years from now. We inevitably adapt and evolve as we move along our respective paths and so does the relationship itself. Circumstances continually change, putting pressure on connection in any type of relationship.

> Successful connection requires a deep integration of each soul as one, for it is the one aspect of our being that will never change.

Our bodies mature, our minds atrophy, and even our hearts lose connection from time to time, but it is our souls that evolve, adapt and stay true throughout the course of our path, fulfilling our contract for eternity. We must take our time in love, for the integrity and longevity are dependent upon its foundation. A true friendship or romantic relationship designed to last requires a powerful foundation with firm support structures and compatible morals and values for the duration of the relationship.

> Life is not a race; we move through this existence at the precise pace and speed of destiny, as everything works out exactly as it is so designed.

We must invest in the foundation of every relationship, simultaneously giving the relationship and the parties involved the space and support they need to continue to evolve and develop.

Lessons for Longevity

Prayer is when you talk to God;
meditation is when you listen to God.
—Diana Robinson

- When in the heat of an argument or when experiencing our inner demons, why do we feel the need to spew the trite thoughts of our petty intellect to those we love, often inflicting tremendous damage?
- Why can it be challenging to create personal time in the midst of a committed relationship or family?

EVERY SUCCESSFUL RELATIONSHIP IS BUILT UPON A STRONG, carefully crafted foundation. The creation and maintenance of a powerful foundation includes a wide range of elements, but it primarily includes a commitment from both parties to their own individual growth and to success of the relationship itself.

- On the rare occasions that we disagree, letting our partner win or be right escalates us above our ego and is a clear choice of love over conflict.

- When we are upset or in a bad space, closing our mouths and reconnecting with Spirit is the only solution that avoids harming our connection to those we love.

- We must create our own existence outside the relationship, and make sure our two lives are still able to successfully merge.

- Clear communication is key to the health of a quality relationship, and our ability to clearly communicate our passions and desires is just as important as our ability to share our love.

- As individuals in a relationship, it is important for both parties to have the time and space they require for their own personal intimacy with Spirit or God. In a healthy relationship, personal time will increase both parties' desire for the other and increase the potential for new and exciting experiences.

- We mustn't try to save old, dying friendships and relationships unless there is value to be shared. Most times, the emotional injuries are too deep to heal even the most intuitive and loving of friendships.

- Having children is a lifetime contract, and we must ensure our children constant sanctuary, regardless of the state of the relationship. In the heat of conflicts with our partner, we cannot underestimate the irreparable harm that comes from putting our children in the middle.

- We must remember what is most important in our lives, for there are always opportunities to focus on areas outside the relationship, but if we take our relationships for granted, they will eventually dissipate.

- There is always an opportunity to give a special something to the one we love, especially when least expected.

- We can never fully say how much we love our partner or tell our loved ones that that we love them too often.

- Just as we require personal quiet time for spirituality and evolution, our intimate relationship requires the same. We must take quiet, personal getaways on a regular basis; it keeps our relationship alive, loving, and fluid.

- We must accept and love our partner's imperfections. We must accept and love them for the fullness of their being; for their weaknesses, and for their greatness. Our ability to fully love our partner is a reflection of our ability to accept and love ourselves.

We cannot take our most important relationships for granted, whether with ourselves or our loved ones. Fulfilled relationships require time, commitment, and an incredible level of honesty, kindness, love, and trust.

- Happiness and fulfillment are available to all of us in every moment and in every relationship. It is up to us to consciously choose happiness in every decision we make.

Intuition & True Love

One joy scatters a hundred griefs.
—Chinese Proverb

- Why do we take our spouse or loved ones for granted?
- Why do we look for the perfect partner, only to settle for companionship, mediocrity, and pettiness?
- Why do we practice ignorance by seeing pettiness in lieu of greatness?
- Why can't we accept people for who they are?

FINDING THAT SPECIAL SOMEONE TENDS TO BE ONE OF OUR most important priorities and most significant decisions in our life. We are choosing the person with whom we share every aspect of our existence, our greatest joys, and our deepest fears. We are choosing the person with whom we will share the expansion of our species. With this person, through our love, we may have children and dedicate the most significant allocation of our heart, soul, and existence.

- How do we know when we have found *the one*?

How do we ever really know? Is it similar to looking for a job by scouring the want ads? How much do we negotiate? How do we maintain our composure and keep from looking too desperate or needy? Do we take whatever job is available to us in the moment, or do we hold out for the perfect one? Do we choose our partner because they are the best option in the moment, or are they the one we are meant to share our life with?

> Perhaps it is our distorted concept of eternity that makes the decision more complicated than necessary.

Some are blessed with an incredible ability to recognize "true love," or the existence of an astounding and soul-based connection, instantaneously. Others struggle, looking for signs to support either the existence or termination of an otherwise less than satisfactory relationship. Beyond intimacy, the same clarity and intuition that is utilized for true love is utilized for partnership, friendship, and every other connection in life. Intuition alone is never enough, for we must have clarity of focus in what we seek in order to receive the guidance of Spirit to assist us in our goals. Once we have clarity, we must listen to our intuition and follow the guidance.

> Just as we listen to our "gut instinct" to keep us out of harm's way, that same guidance helps us obtain what we desire in all areas of our life.

People are merely conglomerations of energy, and the connections two people share is an extension of that energy. Attracting the people we desire is a matter of understanding what we desire and sending that message out into the universe, using the tools available to us to attract what we desire. We cannot control the free will or behaviors of others, but we can utilize the greatness within ourselves in every moment.

> It is our clarity, our vision, and the outward expression of our own greatness combined with our connection to Spirit that attracts us to another.

When we become attached to those who do not share our feelings or love, we must let go of our agenda and stay open to what is available. Although we have a tendency to forget or get caught up in the disappointment of the moment, there is a reason for everything and we must trust in that knowledge. In hindsight and with time, we will see that everything that has ever happened has occurred exactly as it was destined. Outside of intimacy, it is that same level of clarity, focus, intention, and intuition that guides all aspects of our reality, ensuring that we are connecting to the right people at the right time, for all that we require and everything we desire.

~ We must be the quality of person we desire to attract.

If we choose not to take care of ourselves, why attempt to attract someone who does? We need not pretend to be someone we are not, for illusions quickly fade. We must simply put forth the greatness we are. It is through our strength that we attract and invite the greatness in another, and it is that connection that creates the strongest bond from one to another.

~ It is our ability to see the greatness in another that provides the foundation for friendship, relationship, intimacy, and even true love.

When Relationships Fail

Why do you hasten to remove anything which hurts your eye,
while if something affects your soul
you postpone the cure until next year?
—Horace

- Why do we desire to create permanency in relationship?
- Why don't all relationships last forever? Should they?
- How is it possible for two people in a long-term relationship to evolve at the same pace?
- Why do we stay in a miserable or abusive relationship? Why is it so difficult to jump from a sinking ship?

When we fall in love, we talk about eternity; when we get married, traditionally we say, "till death." When were we granted the ability to predict our life's future or that of another? Why do we pretend to know what the future may hold? A commitment to a relationship is only a commitment of the moment, for no other moment truly exists.

~ We can pretend to put forth commitments toward a future we may never see, but we are wasting our breath. This moment is the only one honoring our commitments.

What is it about intimate relationships that causes us to feel the need to make them last forever? Perhaps a specific relationship is for a certain purpose, and as a result, we are in it until we learn a particular lesson. Relationships will fail more often than they succeed, merely as a function of our goals to better ourselves and our commitment to finding the right relationship for our lives in any given moment. When relationships don't work, the impacts can be seen far and wide, as we deal with the emotional anguish and the pain of evolution and change. In the face of such adversity, some of us will crash and others may rise to the occasion. Some of us go inside for the healing we require; others step outside for a respite from the pain. Some of us may seek physical release from the pain, and others seek a more spiritual release.

~ We all deal with the challenges of our existence in different ways, but it is our ability to transcend obstacles through higher levels of consciousness that provides us the opportunity to evolve.

Relationships will fail; it is inevitable. Just as we change jobs or careers over time, just as our neighbors change, our relationships will evolve as well. There is perfect equilibrium in all things, and as a result, balance will be found in one way or another, within our current situation or outside of it, within us or outside of us. But that knowledge is no excuse for poor judgment. A troubled relationship is not an excuse for having an affair; but it may be a symptom of the real issue. Smoking and drinking are not plausible solutions for a stressful life, even though they are often symptoms of internal imbalance. Taking drugs is not the answer for healing inner pain and struggle but is a temporary solution used by some to take respite from the truth.

~ We must face the truth of our lives instead of hiding behind ignorance or evasion.

We must be honest with ourselves in making the changes required to find the lasting happiness we desire and deserve. We must take responsibility for our decisions to ensure that we are respecting our own wishes and inner truth. Decisions that are made out of alignment with our purpose are those that ignore the truth and force change upon ourselves. When relationships aren't working for one person, there is no way they can be working for the other. This is true in intimacy as well as in every relationship in our life.

> If the needs of the relationship are not fulfilling both parties, then the relationship is not fulfilling its purpose.

When a relationship isn't working, why do we stay in it? Are we unable to make changes on our own? Life is too short to stay in a situation that we know is wrong, for that is inconsistent with who we are. We must release each other to our own evolution, letting go of the past and moving forward. When relationships aren't working, we must get out quickly, minimizing any further detrimental impact it may have on our lives and that of our partner.

> The sooner we make the difficult decisions, the sooner we step into our future and into our greatness.

We must have the courage to change those aspects of our lives that are out of balance, without happiness, or not in alignment with our truth and purpose for being. Balance will be found again eventually. We will either consciously or subconsciously make changes for the betterment of ourselves and our community or be forced into change by conditions outside of our control.

> If we don't sabotage ourselves, we will evolve, transcending our current reality to become the person we desire, with or without the people currently a part of our life.

Children

Are children a gift or an obligation?

Can children ever be an ACCIDENT*?*

Do children have a deeper connection to their source then we do?

Do we rush the evolution of our children?

Children's Commitment

God hides things by putting them all around us.
—Author Unknown

- When do our children become an obligation?
- Why do we use the term "accidents" when justifying the arrival of a soul upon this earth?
- Are there really any accidents?

HAVING CHILDREN IS A LIFETIME COMMITMENT AND A DECIsion nobody can make for us, though the Universe will often lend a hand. The responsibilities and daily tasks can overwhelm reason, yet the smiles, beauty, and magnificence of children tantalize all heart's desires. The decision to have a child cannot be made by others, for it is an agreement between a child's soul and ours as they consciously choose to enter this world through the opportunity we extend. Spiritually, there is a decision, an agreement, a contract made on the part of all involved parties. A child chooses his parents for the lessons or opportunities presented, and the parents choose the child in order that they also have the opportunity for growth and evolution. We are powerful beings in full control of our own destiny—and there are no accidents.

- We are responsible for the creation of every aspect of our existence, including and especially the children we bring into this world.

Other than total abstinence, no birth control is 100% effective. So when *accidents* ensue, we must take a moment to accept that there really are no accidents, that everything happens as it is supposed to. That being said, we do have free will, and as such, we are the determinant of our reality. We are not obligated to move forward with the birth of a child. It is an opportunity to bring a child into this world because of the incredible love we are able to share. A soul entering this world surrogates through the parents as a distinct part of their divine plan.

- Once we have brought a child into this world, our only path is to welcome and love that child with all our soul.

Children share an energetic field with their mother when they are born, and that connection is paramount, as it supports the soul's transition into our physical experience. But with our dual-income society, our children are often raised as much or more by their school system, extended family, the television, or even their peer group. Are our children lacking in consistent connection to their mothers or fathers?

- Children are often the reflection we require to guide us, to show us what is important along our path.

We cannot control our children, and as we attract what we fear, oftentimes it is what we fear that we manifest in our children. Many times the lessons before us are presented through our children or as a factor of our relationship with them. The learning we experience through our children allows us to become all that we are able.

- We don't necessarily need to like our children all of the time, but we can love them eternally.

Accepting our children fully is to love them without recourse, without judgment, and regardless of the decisions they make. We can accept our children exactly as they are. We may not like them all the time, nor will we approve of all of their decisions. But irrespective of the choices they make, we can love them just the same.

~ As parents we do our best, and as with all of life, we can only leave the rest to the Universe.

A Child's Wisdom

Man's main task in life is to give birth to himself,
to become what he potentially is.
The most important product of his effort is his own personality.
—Erich Fromm

- What makes a baby or child so precious and magical?
- Is it the perception of their intimate connection to their soul or Higher Consciousness?
- Is it because they have so much to teach us or that we have so much to learn?

WE GIVE BIRTH TO A CHILD AND TEACH THEM ASPECTS OF reality, guiding them through life's challenges and tribulations. As their soul slowly enters their body, they become wholly conscious beings, to the point where they fully integrate into this physical plane. Throughout this process, they act as our teachers as they guide and help us discover our own truth in the most challenging of circumstances. Through our interactions with them, they are mirrors, showing us aspects of ourselves and giving us the opportunity to express compassion, acceptance, and love.

~ Children teach us patience, understanding, trust, and allow us to experience the entire gamut of human emotion.

As we age and our children become adults, the circle of life continues as they have the opportunity to experience parenthood themselves and continue their own internal growth as a result. Many times, our children maintain a greater level of understanding about this world, a higher wisdom that surpasses everything we have taught them, and they become even brighter stars within this world. Our natural fate is to follow our parents, allowing our children to teach us, to show us the way to our source that we may have forgotten or felt unable to maintain.

~ As our soul begins to slowly transgress this physical plane, we require more guidance than ever, and it is often our children who provide the guidance we seek.

A child's innocence is magical. There is much to learn and be appreciative of in watching the transition of a soul into the body of humankind, beginning as an infant, through adolescence and into adulthood. We watch their learning, their understandings and even their hard lessons from such an early age. The circle of life is a miraculous process, and our contributions are never lost. What we learn through experience in our lives, beginning as children and on into adulthood, we have the opportunity to impart to another generation. We hope to help them avoid the trials and tribulations that we experienced ourselves. We realize, of course that the very trials and tribulations we experienced helped to define who we became in this life, and our children have their own share of obstacles and challenges. The circle continues eternally as our children take our place and assist their offspring with their own transition.

- There is always much to learn and much to share, as long as we stay open to our own personal evolution and to that which we can impart to others.

Children & Growth

I am convinced all of humanity is born
with more gifts than we know.
Most are born geniuses and just get de-geniused rapidly.
—Buckminster Fuller

- When raising children, why are we in such a hurry?
- Why do we complain about the very experiences that make us sad in retrospect?
- Why are we upset when our children don't turn out exactly the way we "wanted" them to? Do we blame ourselves?

IN REARING A CHILD, IT SEEMS THAT WE ARE ALWAYS AWAITING the next positive change, their next step in the evolutionary process, the moment when they stop doing the things that drive us crazy. We wait for them to grow, yet for every skill they gain, there is part of their childhood that they subsequently lose. As an infant, they are dependent upon us for all things. As a baby learns the smallest fundamentals, like rolling over or sitting up, they are suddenly slightly less dependent on our assistance for their existence. As they learn to crawl, use a fork, drink by themselves, or walk, they get a taste of freedom. They discover being in control, going where they want, investigating, and exploring. A child is suddenly free to terrorize, wreak havoc, and conquer their world—and ours. No longer can we merely set them down on the carpet and turn our backs. No longer can we put them in bed, say goodnight, and get them out of bed the next morning.

> ~ All of a sudden the joys of evolution coincide with their letting go of the elements of childhood.

As human beings, we have been trained to work toward the future, looking forward to what is yet to come. For some, that is all we live for. As parents, we find ourselves looking forward to the day our children are able to walk, read, write, engage in conversation, clean up after themselves, get dressed in the morning, make their own breakfast, and even do their own laundry. We await the time when they are responsible for their own decisions, when they can drive themselves from place to place, when they have a job, a home of their own, and can take care of themselves.

> ~ All of a sudden, as if instantaneously, our children are no longer dependent upon us. They become adults and even parents themselves.

We are suddenly faced with the hard reality of wondering if we were fully present when we needed to be, if we spent enough quality time with them, or if we worked too much and missed out on core opportunities. We wonder if we made the right decisions, chose the right schools, and taught them respect, honesty, and integrity. We wonder if we could have done more or been a better parent. We wonder if we could take back the times that we lost our temper or said things that we didn't mean.

- Time is short. Soon we will recall the times that traumatized us the most, the times that taught our children boundaries and independence, times that still bring us smiles and a soul's appreciation.

We must let them go. We cannot carry their burden; we must simply release them to the greatness that they are. We wake up one morning and accept the reality that we did our very best. We are all human, and we make mistakes as a natural progression of life itself. Yet everything turned out exactly the way it was supposed to. We fully appreciate, perhaps for the first time, that our children are perfect. We did our job and can be proud not only of our children, who turned out exactly how they were supposed to, but of ourselves as well.

- Every moment is an opportunity to connect with our children, no matter what age they are or what stage of life they are going through.

Our children are here for us as much as we are here for them. They are here to teach us, guide us and help us evolve into better beings. Children help us connect with our deepest emotions. They help us understand ourselves and assist us with our compassion, understanding, empathy, the ability to let go, and most importantly, the remarkable power of true love.

- Children are our teachers; they give us the opportunity to stay true to ourselves and to our life purpose.

Family & Parenting

How do we teach freedom while keeping our children safe?

Do we over-parent our children?

Do we choose to be right over maintaining our heart connection?

Do we give our children the opportunity to become the fullness of themselves?

Boundaries & Freedom

We do not deal much in facts
when we are contemplating ourselves.
—Mark Twain

- Why do some parents have such a difficult time setting boundaries for their children?
- How do we give our children freedom while also giving them healthy boundaries?
- How do we educate them to make the right decisions?

Building a parent-child relationship is as much about boundaries as it is about freedom. The respect that is created between a parent and child develops as a result of the character of the individuals in relation to the roles they play. A parent who chooses to be a friend instead of a parent will rarely develop the respect required for the relationship to operate as it was intended. A parent needs the respect of the child in order to teach, educate, and of course keep the child out of harm's way. By having respect for the parent, a child is able to accept and acknowledge what is being taught as right from wrong, as good from bad.

> Children will not listen to everyone, only to those they perceive of significance—whether through their position, activities, appearance, or merely as who they present themselves.

Without the guidance of a parental figure, a child will look elsewhere for the direction and leadership they require. We are unable to control whether our child learns from a teacher at school or a gang leader on the street, but we do have the ability to guide, love, and support our children in their greatness. We have little say whether our child seeks positive wisdom from the school bus driver or learns "right" from our neighbors down the street.

> We not only have the opportunity but the requirement to be the role models our children deserve in their lives.

We must guide and assist our children in their freedom and in their structure so that they develop and become their greatness, the fullness of themselves. By bringing children into this world, whether by choice or "accident," we are obligated to provide for their needs in the physical realm and in the emotional and spiritual ones as well, however and whenever possible.

> However sudden the actual action of impregnation may seem, the commitment to bring a child into this world is eternal.

Good Parenting

Don't worry that children never listen to you;
worry that they are always watching you.
—Robert Fulghum

- What do our children truly require?
- With no guidebook or instruction manual, how can we become the best parents for our children?
- How do we avoid getting angry or frustrated?
- Is it possible to stay in a place of love?

WE CAN ALL CONCEPTUALIZE THE ASPECTS THAT MAKE A good parent, perhaps as reflections of those traits that make up a bad one. Desired traits may include spending quality time, being a positive and supportive role model, deepening our connection, and fostering the greatness of our children. We may not exactly agree on the most important elements of a good parent, but we might agree on the traits that typify an immoral or absentee parent: a shortage of supply in any of our children's core needs, whether emotional, physical, spiritual, or psychological abuse, a negative environment, etc.

- Children learn more from who we are than by what we say or attempt to teach or preach.

We can become better parents; there is always room for improvement. We may see and get frustrated by our children's glorious imperfections, but eventually we realize that they are simply reflections of the pain or lack within ourselves. We look deep within ourselves to find the truth of our own parent-child connection, and many times what we find is not what we had expected. We often see the truth within ourselves, of which we may have been previously in denial. We experience aspects of our children, and as a result become conscious to the replay of our lives many years in passing. There are always times when we can be more loving, extra caring, and more deeply connected, but we must be careful not to blame our children for the pain we experience in our own lives.

- We can all be more supportive, nurturing, loving, and engaged.

Quality time is a good place to start as our children generally require a greater amount of focus than we think, but there is no right or wrong amount of time. We adapt on a daily basis as to what we give and receive, as do our children, thus compounding the complexity of our interaction and interrelatedness. We underestimate the characteristics of our parents that frustrated us as children and that we subsequently infused into our role as parents.

- We often don't realize the way we act toward our offspring, not seeing them for who they truly are in our lives and in the world at large.

Our children are perfect. They are everything they are destined to be. Our role is to provide for them, guide them, and love them. We are here to nurture their greatness, support them in finding and following their own truth and discovering their inner compass. Our children didn't come here to follow in our footsteps—they are here to create their own.

~ By being ourselves, following our truth, and providing unconditional love to our children, we cannot fail.

Child's Connection

A child's life is like a piece of paper
on which every person leaves a mark.
—Chinese Proverb

- Why do we often struggle to connect with our children?
- Why is it so hard to enter their world emotionally, physically, or even spiritually?
- Why do we wait for them to enter our word for connection?

WE ALL INHERENTLY KNOW AND UNDERSTAND THAT ABOVE and beyond physical connection and spending time with our children, the bond we share and nurture is primary and essential. When connecting with children, especially as they move through adolescence, we have a tendency to use excuses to explain our lack of connection, even complaining that we have little in common. Connection isn't only about inviting others into our world, but we must enter our children's world in order to connect with them on their level. When they are young, connection can be as simple as getting out of our chair, sitting on the floor, and supporting the fancies of their wildest imaginings.

As our children move into their teenage years, it becomes even more essential to step out of our comfort zone to support and nurture our connection.

- Stepping out of our comfort zone and into that of our children's creates the greatest opportunity for connection.

As our children continue to mature, our relationship is not about our life or our path or even any specific agenda. We are here to support the path and destiny of our children, wherever it may take us. In that respect, our level of service can feel unidirectional. But service comes in many forms, and its display may come in the form of inaction as we allow our children to stand on their own two feet and even learn to pick themselves up when they fall.

- The gift we receive through service can fill the depths of our heart and soul, far exceeding any level of fulfillment we can receive in any other aspect of our lives.

We table our plans and timelines and just connect with our children however that may be available to us in any particular moment. This is not to say that we sacrifice our existence or eliminate boundaries, but when it comes time to connect, it is the all and everything, it is the only thing that matters within the present moment. True connection is golden. During these special times, we must be sure to eliminate all distractions, whether through music, cell phones, or other interruptions in order to give our children the full attention they deserve. The extra effort required to make ourselves available for our children is the reason we invited them here in the first place.

- When connecting with our hearts, it doesn't matter where we are, what we are talking about, or what we are doing.

Quality time comes in different forms. As adults we have a tendency to place structure around even the simplest of interactions, overly complicating what is at its core—a heart-to-heart connection between parent and child. Often, it is the parent who lacks the maturity to realize and take responsibility for their aspect of the relationship and blames the child or teenager for being difficult or for not being available or present for the connection. But we need to remember that we can only control ourselves, that we have only ourselves to blame for the state of our lives.

~ What our children require is simple: an unequivocal commitment from us to give them whatever they require by way of nurturing, loving, caring and mentoring—until such time as we are unable.

Balance & Children

Not until we are lost do we begin to understand ourselves.
—Henry David Thoreau

- Do we know the right way to raise a child? Do we know the wrong way?
- Are we over-protective of our children?
- Why is it challenging to give children the space to grow while at the same time giving them the boundaries they require?
- Don't we realize that they need to make their own mistakes in order to evolve and grow?

WE WALK A FINE, ETERNAL LINE BETWEEN LOOKING OUT FOR the safety of our children, and giving them the freedom to discover life for themselves and finding their own associated lessons. We have all seen or experienced parents of both extremes, those who over-protect their children to the point that they have no independent decision-making ability, and those who give their children full and unabated freedom as if they were fully functioning adults. With over-protection, a parent-child dynamic is created that puts the child in a situation of total dependence upon our guidance for every aspect of their lives. In this particularly extreme case, we create children in our ego's mind and likeness who always need and make us feel as if we are always needed. We get to be the hero, the savior, the rescuer, and the abuser.

> ~ We create a role for ourselves whereby we pretend to look out for the best interests of our children when, in fact, the actual focus is on our own personal needs.

In the alternative, there are those parents who have no boundaries, who let their children do anything, watch everything with the freedom to discover the world at any age. Their motto is one of "I want my children to experience everything." These children may watch stereotypically inappropriate movies, test vices far too early, and carelessly dive into the world with two very unbalanced feet. These children set their own schedules, may be responsible for making their own meals, and even setting their own bedtime. These children generally live in homes where their parents don't have enough time or interest to teach, impart, or participate in their development process; or perhaps they believe that freedom is what is best. These parents have generally either thrown their hands up in exhaustion and frustration or genuinely believe that their children are better off with them not around. These parents may be extremely lazy, obsessed workaholics, entirely aloof as to the proper care and nurturing of a child, or somehow believe that their children are ready to care for themselves.

> ~ In these two extremes, it is the children who loses, for either way they are deprived of the deep connection they desire and require with their parents.

Children require freedom within the confines of healthy boundaries. We provide them a safe haven in which to grow and learn, an area of love and support to mature into the fullness of themselves. Our children require the freedom to learn, to solve their own problems whenever possible, and to slowly but surely discover the mental, physical and emotional aspects of this human experience. By providing our children with healthy boundaries, we help them develop faith and trust in their own path and abilities. We do our part to share our wisdom and knowledge in a manner and method consistent with the natural process of a child's becoming. We do the job we are here to do—caring for and nurturing our children—in a manner and method consistent with their needs and development. The true role of parenting is selfless service—in the beginning, middle, and end. However, we know it's not truly selfless, for the gift of parenthood is the service we provide.

> ~ We have a lifelong commitment to the magnificence of the children we bring forth into this world.

We love our children and will do anything for them. It is our duty to protect them, yet over-protection of our children does more harm than good. By preventing them from having access to what is available to them in the world, we block them from the experiences they require to evolve individually and collectively. Just as an animal bred in captivity will not know how to protect and feed itself in the wild, a child in extreme confinement will lack survival instincts and access to their intuitive skill set. We must allow our children to fall so that they learn to pick themselves up. In addition, there is a dynamic within some parents who seem to have a requirement to be needed at the expense of their children. Feeling loved and needed by our community is a natural aspect of this existence, yet our children do not deserve to carry our burden. Our children require a certain aspect of independent thinking in order to foster their own existence, thus supporting a manner intended for healthy relationships.

> ~ Children should never carry our burdens as they grow into adulthood, for they have burdens of their own.

Just as a plant needs space to grow and the nutrients and water to support that growth, children require the same in order to flourish as they are destined. Many animals and fish held in captivity will grow only as large as their environment allows. As parents, our role is to support the evolution of our children in addition to giving them the space they require to become their own independent beings. We are here to assist them, to support and encourage them in following their dreams. Of their own accord, they follow their life path in perfect alignment and evolve exactly according to the pace of their unique destiny.

- Our role is one of support, even though our ego appreciates a more hierarchical solution.

Our role is to help them reconnect with their truth, to help them trust their intuition, and to teach them to access their inner wisdom whenever they desire guidance. In a fully supportive relationship, we are here to guide and share, love and respect, for in the end our children become exactly who they are destined to be. We are eternally the parents who brought them into this world and did our job to the best of our ability.

- Regardless of how our children are judged by society, they are on their path, and they are perfect.

Truth

How do we know what's real?

Is the voice we hear the pettiness of our mind or the wisdom of our soul?

When do we learn to trust ourselves?

Is there really a point to this life?

Are we ready to be honest with ourselves?

Genuine Honesty

Honesty is the first chapter of the book of wisdom.
—Thomas Jefferson

- Do we inherently know the answers for which we seek?
- Why do we need confirmation from others for what we innately know to be true?
- Do others somehow instinctively understand our dreams and desires better than we do?
- Why do we pretend to be someone we are not?

BEING HONEST WITH OTHERS IS HARD ENOUGH, BUT SEEING the truth and being honest with ourselves is one of the most difficult challenges we face. Intuitively, we know the right answer, the correct decision, the divine path. Acceptance of that inner knowing is difficult in a culture of interdependence where we have been taught to seek guidance from the outside and rarely from within. If we listened to our intuition, to our soul's wisdom, and accepted the reality of the guidance we were given, the inevitable would not be as complicated, difficult, or painful. We can accept the divine path as it is provided to us and focus our efforts where we can affect positive change within our greater world.

> ~ When we hope the inevitable will change, we only end up frustrated and disappointed, yet move through the lesson regardless.

Life is humorous in that manner, as the very best of intentions, whether wrong or right, will result in the same outcome. We will all lose the battle to live, for it is predetermined. Being honest with those we love and care for is hard enough, yet being honest with ourselves is an entirely different animal. We push our relationships to the limit in the sharing of our intimate feelings, fears, concerns, hopes, and dreams. When we are forced to accept the same level of intimacy within ourselves, it is almost too much to handle. Often experiencing catastrophic illness or witnessing the death of someone we care for has a way of forcing us to re-evaluate our lives so that we make changes for the better. Putting our lives through a microscope, we can easily identify the things we should change. Having the courage to change requires believing in our greatness and that we and our life path are worth the effort. Why would we let anyone stand in the way of our dreams, our happiness, and our purpose?

> ~ We owe it to ourselves to follow our dreams and our path and to listen to our truth, for the pettiness and complacency with which we live is not only disappointing, it is unacceptable.

We cannot recreate any moment within this existence. We will live our truth or we will live a lie, for there is no grey area on a path of purpose. We are either living or dying. We are either following our path or are poor excuses for pure human manifestation in this physical existence. The truth is within us, and accessing it is as simple as asking for the answers and listening.

- Honoring our truth is fulfilling our purpose, and being of service to our loved ones and to our greater communities.

When we wake up in the morning and prepare for the day, we must be able to look into the mirror and fully love the person reflected before us. We must look directly into our soul and accept as truth that we have done everything possible to grow, learn, and live an incredible life. We must know that we have chosen every opportunity to better ourselves, to become more evolved, and to live a life of service as a powerful contributor to this world. When we wake, we recognize that we are a being of conscious choice. We not only accept the reality that we have co-created, but we take responsibility for it as well. When we crawl into bed at night, we accept that we did everything possible to make the world a better place, even if it requires caring for ourselves so that we have the energy to invest in the coming day.

- As we move through life, we must live a life of truth, reflective of the truth we hold within.

We are more empathic than we give ourselves credit for, as we are able to see and feel beyond what is spoken, just as others can see through our insincerity. We need not be hurtful to others, but through insincerity we inevitably do just that. By pretending to be someone we are not, in essence we present a false front, inviting distrust, disrespect and a falsification of who we are. We must give our world exactly what it desires—to live a life of impeccable integrity. We need not be afraid to showcase exactly who we are; the good, the great, and the magnificent.

- A life of service and integrity requires more than merely showing up for life; it requires a commitment to truth in all areas of our existence, for honesty is the only path to happiness.

The Void Within

If you don't get lost,
there's a chance you may never be found.
—Author Unknown

- Why is it so difficult to live our truth?
- Why do we struggle to be our authentic self?
- What stands in the way of our fullest expression?

LIVING OUR TRUTH CAN EVADE EVEN THE MOST ADVANCED among us, and yet it is the most important aspect of our physical existence. We often live as if our lives were predetermined and predestined, as if we didn't need to take responsibility. We pretend that chartered seas have been prescribed for our own existence, our own destiny. The truth is that we are the captains of our own ship; our destiny is ours and ours alone. An awareness of our true existence, a life consistent with our truth, gives way to the pain and strife, allowing us to adapt and evolve for the betterment of ourselves and our greater communities.

~ The fire within us is self-infused, fueled by our desire for greatness, our commitment to our truth and purpose, and our responsibility to our greater world.

Most people would give anything for the world we have currently manifested for ourselves—except when we are in our moments of rediscovery. We can be duplicitous and almost schizophrenic in our lives. In one moment, we provide exemplary service and extraordinary contribution, bringing happiness and appreciation to all whom we contact. We are temporarily "happy" as a result of the positive influence we have brought to the world and grateful for the life we are living. Moments later, we are distraught and distressed, caught in the crossfire of obstacles and challenges, wondering why our life should continue when for the moment it may appear pointless and devoid of meaning.

~ We fluctuate tremendously as we attempt to find meaning and purpose within every moment.

As we all know, our internal barometers don't fire on all cylinders at all times life cannot be rosy in every moment as that doesn't provide us with the appropriate opportunities for growth. There are times when the positive and opportunistic thoughts of the moment are far from reach. It is during these times, often when at our lowest vibration, we may entertain negative thoughts, even suicidal ones—the desire for exodus and release from the ailments of the moment. These thoughts are merely representations of the moment, and through our quick dismissal, they bring about inevitable changes that determine our fate as we seek the truth that resonates within our soul. We can engage in obsessive-compulsive behavior, reacting to the internal void by over- or under-indulging in sleep, food, alcohol or drugs. We can integrate ourselves into society with dreams of stumbling upon the gem of purpose that will carry us through, and help us find true happiness and fulfillment.

~ We anticipate the moment when all of our desires and dreams will come to fruition, and then we wonder why that moment will be any different from this one in which we have been given the full opportunity to embrace.

Whatever the circumstance, and however painful the moment, it shall pass in time. We have an innate desire to find the answers to an endless spattering of undetermined questions, many of which are simply rhetorical in nature. We often lack the vision to see beyond our own internal strife; we desire to embrace much of what troubles us and stands in the way of the evolution of our society as a whole. The external expressions of success and happiness are superficial; they neither quantify nor qualify human existence.

~ Our mind does not maintain the answers to our truth and path in life; it only provides the tools to help us find the truth within ourselves.

Regardless of our current life expression, we drive ourselves to give more, serve more, be more, and are alternately rewarded with success and pain and ongoing opportunities for gratitude and growth. We dream of a passion so deep, a fire blazing so powerfully within us, that we become enveloped with desire, not only for ourselves, but for our contributions to our society as a whole.

~ We must have faith and continue to make the changes required to evolve into the beings we are meant to be.

We can never find the truth of humanity when we attempt to enlist the forces that repel peace and love, engaging in the hypocrisy and dysfunction of the world. We are exactly where we need to be, now and eternally, and it is the consciousness we exert in any particular moment that assists and guides us in finding the meaning in all things.

Death & Truth

Any fool can count the seeds in an apple.
Only God can count all the apples in one seed.
—Robert H. Schuller

- At what point do we realize that none of this matters?
- What does it take for us to comprehend the limited nature of this physical existence?
- When do we step out of our comfort zone and into one worthy of the fullness of ourselves?

NONE OF THIS REALLY MATTERS, NOT AT ALL. THE END RESULT of life is death, and the faster we move through life, the quicker we die. If we lead an incredible or a magnificent life, or alternatively a miserable failure of a life, it doesn't matter because we will still die. In every moment, we are only one breath away from the future, and one from the past. We are one breath away from destroying our lives, and one from living the life of our dreams. We are one breath away from fear, and one from love. And we are always one breath away from death. So what is the purpose of this physical life, and why does any of it matter?

- In order to understand and experience the fullness of life, we must understand and accept the beauty and inevitability of death.

Death defies all odds, for it is the one element of our temporal reality that supersedes all else, the one aspect of our existence that lives almost entirely outside of our control—in reality, not in concept. We can struggle with financial hardship, relationship issues, and simple challenges in this human existence, but suddenly the prospect of death brings it all into perspective.

- When faced with the inevitability of death, everything of prior significance is given up to that which truly matters.

Money can buy many things, but it is unable to reach beyond this physical existence. It has the power to provide for our core physical needs, but beyond the trite necessities, it is powerless to that which really matters, to the void within. Without the distinction of focused intention, money controls our lives, for it is a tangible to which we heed and hold, one that wields much power in this capitalistic society. However, that power is only an illusion, for in the face of death or shortly thereafter, money has no actual or empirical value whatsoever.

- Death supersedes all else when faced with the struggles of our existence.

The life we live determines the quality of our existence, and often it is the inevitability and unpredictability of death that gives us the courage to step beyond our ego and limited mentally into greatness. It is often the prospect of death that provides us the strength to risk embarrassment, to tempt failure, to do that which we have always dreamed but never had the courage to risk. Our life is only what we make of it, but so easily we relent and sacrifice our core values for the needs of the moment.

~ It is often death or the prospect thereof that forces us to face the stark reality or magnificence of our own existence.

Sometimes life feels like one big struggle, from one moment to the next, like we can never catch a break, but it is our inner wisdom and strength that provides us the ability to overcome everything that stands in the way of our greatness and to actualize our goals and dreams. Our external environment is simply an outward reflection of our internal weather. That which can be conceived is quite often far from our reality unless it can be internalized into a manner that engages our emotional and spiritual body. Overcoming our mental anguish is often required for the spectacular, the magnificent, and the truth of our existence. Our lives are reminiscent only of its potentiality; the memories we leave behind are the only breadcrumbs of our existence.

~ In every moment, we are either living or dying.

We can allow the inevitability of death to provide us with the strength to say what needs to be said, do what needs to be done, and live the life we are destined. The world is incomplete without our contributions, however trite they may feel in the moment.

~ The reverberations of service and greatness travel far beyond even our wildest dreams.

Extended Connection

To conquer fear is the beginning of wisdom.
—Bertrand Russell

- What allows us to trust each other?
- Where do we look for true guidance?
- Are we conscious of the people we surround ourselves with?
- Do we understand the impact others play within our circle of influence?
- Do we trust ourselves?

WE OFTEN FORGET THE IMPORTANT ROLE PLAYED BY THOSE within our own various circles of influence. As members of our greater communities, it is those we trust and love the most that often guide us through the treacherous waters, giving us the courage and strength to be more, give more, and to stay true to our path. Many times, it is these small microcosmic communities that affect change most powerfully in our society. Sometimes our most powerful circle of influence is made up of our dearest friends or coworkers, and other times it's our loved ones or extended family.

> ~ As much as anything else, it is our support network within this physical reality that assists us in finding the clarity we require.

As much as we can grow and foster positive contribution, sometimes it is these very communities that become a detriment to our lives. Just as a recovering alcoholic should find situations and relationships that support his or her sobriety, we need to surround ourselves with people and situations that support our dreams and desires. As we move forward and evolve, we are often guided to let go of those who stand in the way of our greatness. It is very noble to be diplomatic or egalitarian, but at the end of the day, we must look out for ourselves and those closest to our heart. When those we trust, respect, or love change their method of contribution and put us in situations that cause harm to ourselves or to those we are here to protect, we must make the changes necessary to ensure our safety.

> ~ Just as we can accept the positive contributions of another, we can also accept their pain, negativity, and the limitations within their own existence.

Harm can arrive in a myriad of ways, not merely in physical form, but also emotionally and spiritually. It is our role to stand up for ourselves and for those closest to our heart. Oftentimes, stern and clear communication can ease the sovereign intellect when in a place of disagreement; but in the end, we must make the often painful decision as to whether certain people should continue within our personal circle of influence. Distancing ourselves from those we love in order to protect those we have sworn to shield is not disrespectful and is not mean; it is our job—it is our duty.

> ~ Everyone needs to be loved, but when love comes with a price, it isn't really love.

The communities we create, whether by birth or by choice, can have the greatest influence on our success or our failure. It is our role as caretakers, in respect of our soul and life purpose, to make the often difficult decisions to stay true to ourselves and to those we serve. There is much to be gained by surrounding ourselves with those who are able to be of service to us and with us. In balance, we give back in service to our communities, as we distance ourselves from those contrary to the vision and path we maintain for ourselves, allowing us to maintain our healthy equilibrium.

~ The healthier we get, the harder it is to keep sick people in our life.

Nothing Really Matters

There cannot be a God because
if there were one, I could not believe that I was not He.
—Friedrich Nietzsche

- Do our possessions really matter?
- Do our family and friends actually matter?
- Does anything really matter in the end?
- What is the significance of our very existence? What is the point of this life?

NOTHING IN LIFE REALLY MATTERS—NOT ANY OF IT, NOT even a little bit. The significance of anything is only what we make of it. First and foremost, we are simple beings looking from the inside out. This is not a flaw; it is merely the way we have been designed to operate—to look at the world through rose-colored glasses, as if our proprietary perception has anything whatsoever to do with that of anyone else's. We are unique in that we are designed to be selfish; we are built to lookout for ourselves first and others second.

- We must get past ourselves and into the realm of truth. We must find source within and seek spirituality and truth through each and every experience, with each and every soul around us.

Our lives are reflections of the trials and tribulations of our soul. What we experience within is what we reflect in our lives, for the chaos of our life is a mirror image of the chaos within. If we fix our lives from the inside out, we enjoy the reflection from the outside in. At some point, we realize that we cannot change what we actually experience within our lives, but only our perceptions and beliefs that give our experience meaning. We can exert all of our energy and that of the Universe to correct what we determine requires our attention; yet we are still faced with the same challenge of going within to find that which we seek, as that is the only place where anything has meaning.

- When our lives are a disaster on the outside, the only option we have is to re-discover the truth and the reality within, knowing that it will correct the reality without.

The basis for a world indebted to our higher spirit requires a level of trust and respect that lives beyond the sovereign intellect, a level beyond our personal comprehension. We ask for help with our sanctity and trust that the answers will help us find the clarity to make the changes required to become healthy, happy, and fulfilled individuals. Let us not forget that irrespective of our circumstance, we can breathe easy because in the end none of this matters, not one bit.

- Whether or not we see them, the signs in our life are a reflection of our ability to connect with our soul and with the Universe itself.

We will all experience a physical death. Our soul will transcend place and time to our next destination, and still—none of this matters. All of the stress, lessons, pain, struggle, chaos, and even happiness, joy, peace, and sadness will all be left behind as we reconnect with the core of our being to accept our next assignment.

~ We must not take it all so seriously, for none of it really matters—not for us, not for anyone.

We experience the finest moments and the most traumatic, yet they are one and the same, as they don't even exist in the space and time continuum within the universe itself. We must release it all and let it all go. We are here to live the fullness of life, to express and experience love, and to be of service wherever possible—until it's time to move on. We can get so caught up in life, taking everything so seriously, when in the end, absolutely nothing matters. With the season finale on the reality show of life, we all move on to bigger and better. Somehow, we all evolve and the world becomes a better place. There is no stress in the afterlife, for it is simply a new beginning, the do-over we waited for our entire life.

~ We will all return from whence we came, and we take nothing with us save the development of our character and our soul.

Responsibility

Why do we blame others for our misfortunes?

Do we blame to avoid taking responsibility for our truth?

How do we learn to take responsibility for our actions?

What is faith and how do we find it?

Can anything we truly desire be found outside ourselves?

Choose Life & Take Responsibility

Sell not virtue to purchase wealth,
nor liberty to purchase power.
—Benjamin Franklin

- Why do we move forward through life without taking responsibility for our path, our reality, or the decisions we make along the way?
- Why do we often lie to ourselves and to others, pretending to be people we are not, living our lives in direct opposition to the truth we inherently know?

WHILE MANY PEOPLE MERELY BECOME THEIR LIFE, WE HAVE the opportunity to consciously choose and create it. Oftentimes, the smaller decisions in our lives may lead us to situations that we may not have consciously chosen. Living with regret or disappointment is disastrous over the long-term. With many reasons to exclude ourselves from our current environment, we must choose and accept the choices we have made and our current situation. Our present moment is a reflection of the past, of the choices previously made. Our future is made in the choices of the present moment.

- If necessary, we need to take responsibility for changing our situation rather than blaming it on forces outside our control.

We need to present ourselves to the world as we truly are, as human beings who are connected to our soul and accepting of our own humanity. We must love and appreciate being human even with all of the resulting benefits and ramifications. We must venture forward with a full realization of our role within the manufactured reality that lies ahead, pressing on with pride, responsibility, and focus.

- We must take responsibility for anything and everything that we can control. The rest we can only accept without recourse.

Everyone contemplates personal exodus at some point in time, weighing the alternatives of living the challenges of the human experience or living in mediocrity while attempting to ignore the truth. Departure is truly the only full and all-encompassing alternative we have to facing our lives. Drugs or alcohol can be used to temporarily distract or withdraw from the reality of a given moment, but for lasting release, suicide is the only true alternative to living our life. Is it cowardly? Potentially, but it is an alternative, nonetheless.

- Although we crucify physical suicide, emotional or spiritual suicide can be just as severe.

We need to take a moment to contemplate how far we have come in this lifetime, conquering the many seemingly impossible lessons of life that have challenged our every moral, questioned our every belief, and required us to dig to the center of our being for the lessons and answers we require. We have striven to find answers for those who suffered at our expense and for the gifts to give those who sacrificed everything so that we could have a life worth living. There is only one high road, with a lane for each of us and the opportunity for everlasting happiness, joy, peace, and love; if only we would consistently choose it. Life is not always easy, but it can be magnificent.

- There is honor and pride in becoming the all and everything, in following our truth and becoming ourselves.

Universal Balance

We make a living by what we get,
but we make a life by what we give.
—Winston Churchill

- Why do we blame the world for our woes, struggles, and the perceptions we utilize to create our reality?
- Why do we use our external world as a crutch, as an excuse to express neither our truth nor our greatness?
- Is there balance in the universe?

THIS LEADS TO THE UNDERSTANDING THAT THE ENTIRE world is made up of positive and negative, black and white, good and bad, yin and yang, everything and nothing. Every moment is made up of smiles and sorrow, light and dark, giving and receiving. This immaculate balance allows the opportunity for all emotion to be expressed and experienced within every moment, and it gives all of us the ability to consciously choose our emotions, experiences, and reality. Nothing is forced, coerced, or even predetermined, for it is our reaction to every experience that determines who we are and who we become. As we combine the experiences of our lifetime, we develop our character, a presence, and an ongoing consciousness that follows us not only from moment to moment, but becomes a part of our soul and stays with us through our ongoing evolution.

> The inherent balance of the universe is based upon the ideology that there is perfect balance in everything, not only in perception but in actuality.

We must take responsibility, for there is nobody to blame but ourselves for our role, or lack thereof, as participants in the balance of the universe. The equilibrium of our universe extends far beyond the equal shares of emotion, connection, time, and life that make up our daily life. The balance of the universe is the effervescent commingling of realities that encompasses all things and yet envelops nothing. Just as we have the freedom and choice to experience our life in whatever manner we see fit, there is no judgment in the Universe, regardless of which path we choose.

> Within every instant exists the opportunity to experience the depth or the superficiality of every moment, a reality of our own volition.

Life itself becomes the commitment we make to express our greatness and our glory through triumph and tribulation in every moment, experience, and opportunity available. It is our life itself, our own evolution and consciousness, that communally creates the intricate balance of existence.

> By conscious selection, we choose existence—the engagement in a life of body, mind, and soul through which we become active and committed participants in this world.

Unbending Faith

Faith consists in believing
when it is beyond the power of reason to believe.
—Voltaire

- What is faith?
- How do we learn to believe?
- When are we taught to listen to our inner truth?

As children, we are taught to follow direction—not our inner direction, but our outer direction, the instructions that are handed *to* us. We are taught English, math, foreign language, science, sports, and every aspect of learning that exists outside of ourselves. But when do we learn to listen to our intuition, to hear our truth, and to follow our inner compass?

- When are we taught that the answers we seek, and all that we truly desire, cannot be found outside of ourselves?

We learn to believe in the mystical, magical, and mysterious as we are guided to believe in Superman, Barbie, Batman, Santa Claus, and the tooth fairy. One day, we learn that all of our mystical friends are not real at all, but simply comical aberrations—save one. Even as all of our imaginary friends have been disproved, we are asked to continue our belief in just one of them—God.

- Are we meant to believe in a supernatural being just because our family or friends do?

No child, teenager, or adult likes to be told what to do. So how do we determine our own definition of the universe, spirituality, or what many refer to as God? We must discover it for ourselves—for faith requires an inner knowing that only comes from the confidence of discovery, awareness, and truth.

- Faith is what helps us overcome the obstacles that stand between where we are and where we want to be.

How can we believe in something that cannot be scientifically proven—or disproven—of which Spirit, God, or any higher power technically cannot. How do we explain or prove the existence of love, thoughts, emotions, or ideas? Nothing outside of ourselves can prove or disprove the existence of something within us.

- We are amorphous in nature, as is the energy of the Universe, which flows in and through each and every one of us.

What is this outside power that we often scapegoat? What is the energy behind our reality? If we don't take action in our lives, no amount of praying will resolve what we require. We can pray for a job, but if we don't get off the couch and apply for one, chances are we won't get one. We can pray to relinquish our hunger, but we must choose to eat. We can pray, but we must take action. How passive have we become that we wait for others or the Universe to provide for us?

- We have been given *all* the gifts and tools needed to obtain all that we desire.

God Within

To the question of your life you are the answer,
and to the problems of your life you are the solution.
—Joe Cordare

- Why do we always look for answers outside of ourselves?
- Are we looking everywhere but within when searching for our truth?
- Why do we turn to religion when we long to connect with Spirit, the Universe, or God?

WE HAVE A HABIT OF LOOKING TO EXTERNAL SOURCES FOR the connection we require to our source. We talk to our friends and family, various experts, alleged "representatives" of God or the Universe, essentially looking everywhere but within for the connection we seek. Unfortunately, we cannot find what we seek without looking within ourselves.

- Others can assist us on our path, but we must take every step on our own.

We are not guaranteed nourishment of our soul or connection to God or the Universe simply by visiting our church, synagogue or mosque. Similarly, we cannot improve our mind by walking by a library or strengthen our body by watching others exercise. Working in a church no more makes us a representative of God, than sleeping in our garage makes us an automobile. More time in the gym doesn't necessarily make us stronger, faster, or more flexible. More time in the kitchen doesn't make us a chef, and more time at the office doesn't make us a better employee. We can find our spirituality whenever and wherever we choose to look.

~ A priest, imam, or pastor is no closer to God or Spirit than you or I.

We cannot learn by putting a book under our pillow, and we cannot discover the world without leaving our home. Just as a garden requires preparation of the land, planting of seeds, water, ongoing nourishment and attention, we must nurture, cherish, and cultivate our soul. Our connection to Spirit or the Universe is ongoing and is not a passive experience, for we must consciously choose and connect with that which we desire. However, when it comes to our own path and truth, there is no replacement for our bond to our spirituality, to ourselves. We all maintain the same opportunity for deep and intimate connection to our source and the higher powers of the Universe. Yet it is our acknowledgment of and focus on that relationship and our commitment to living our truth that is the differentiator.

~ Regardless of the information available, we must digest our truth within our own reality.

We must look at the experience before us in the context of a life of meaning, a life that is consciously guided by Spirit or the Universe, one that is in alignment with our life purpose. We can create our own relationship to our source while at the same time nurturing our soul and living the fullness of our life.

~ Nobody can provide us with the answers we seek, for our path is ours alone; and although all paths cross, it is our unique path that differentiates our reality from others.

Petty Blame

Man, at bottom, is not entirely guilty,
since he did not begin history,
nor entirely innocent, since he continues it.
—Albert Camus

- Why do we blame everyone but ourselves for the struggles in our lives?
- Why are we never short of someone or something else to hold responsible for our actions and circumstances?
- Why are we so quick to take responsibility for greatness, but not in its entirety?

WE BLAME THE GOVERNMENT, OUR PARENTS, OUR PEERS, AND even the weather for the challenges in our lives. Instead of taking full responsibility for our actions and outcomes, we blame our environment, education, and the world. We blame anything and everything that might have any involvement whatsoever in our existence. When life is good, it's much easier to take responsibility. Blame is a painful and useless exercise—one of inferiority, inadequacy, and ignorance.

Can our pain be directly attributable to another, or can we plead no contest to the pains of this physical existence? As active participants within this world, we take responsibility for our actions and influence as well as for the pains and joys we integrate into our existence.

- Rarely do we blame those who help us to find our joy, so why do we blame those who instigate or trigger feelings of pain?

In times of need, we require greater support and frequently rely on our Higher Consciousness to assist us through our transition back to greatness. It is often our lower selves, our lower vibrations, that compel us to shift the blame or responsibility to someone else. We live in a world where negativity breeds contempt, manipulation, and coercive behavior, yet positivity breeds nothing but joy, happiness, and goodwill for the common human being. When we listen to our truth, or that of our higher belief system, we rarely exercise a mechanism of defeat because we realize that everything happens for a reason and is a result of the choices we have made throughout our life. We can only hope that all of us may grow conscious and aware of the world around us.

- We can understand and consciously affect positive change, or we can practice ignorance and blame the world around us.

The circle of life is so misunderstood, as if there really was a beginning and an end rather than a continuous cycle of new beginnings and opportunities for transformation and fulfillment. In the context of human life, it is easy to draw boundaries, but the reality of the pre-life and the afterlife is complicated when faced with the opportunity of happiness, love, and peace in this moment. The choice is one of consciousness and assuming responsibility for the magnificence of this existence.

- We are accountable for all of the actions and activities within our world, using our power to manifest that which we know to be true.

Conclusion

There are no facts, only interpretations.
—Friedrich Nietzsche

IN THE END, IT IS THE QUALITY OF OUR LIFE AND NOT THE quantity. There will always be exceptions to every rule, each recommendation, and every aspect of humankind because we are imperfect creatures living in an imperfect world and creating the perfection we call life. We each have the opportunity to control our lives within the boundaries we are given; our happiness is in direct relation to our belief system, which in turn, is the basis for the choices we make and the feelings we experience in every moment. We cannot blame our unhappiness on anyone other than ourselves. Our conclusions, connections, and the entire reality of our existence are controlled by the conscious or unconscious choices we make in every moment.

- We have the right to be happy and deserve to be—but we must choose it and earn it.

We need to give ourselves more credit for being a part of this world and for continuously giving all of ourselves to it. We deserve the fulfillment of our dreams. We merely need to remember the simple guidelines of the life we lead, and in time all of our dreams can be granted.

- Appreciate every moment; continually let go and trust that everything will work out.
- Take responsibility for the choices you make without being too hard on yourself—accept yourself just the way you are.
- Keep life simple; always look for harmony and happiness in all things where possible.
- While focused on your own evolution, make new resolutions as often as possible, for it is positive and supportive of your purpose and passion in life. Then stick with it, at least in this moment, for your life deserves nothing less.
- Practice unconditional love and see your world without prejudice or judgment.
- Find balance in your financial affairs; practice financial wellness and always look for the beauty and spirituality in all things.
- Learn not to take life too seriously; for none of us knows how much time we have left. Stay positive, smile, and always be kind. We can always do what is right in our heart.
- In this moment, appreciate the beauty in all things and all people while living life in moderation and balance.
- As active participants in this world, realize that some are beyond repair and that we will never be able to please everyone.
- Express kindness to those around you while seeking deep and fulfilling connections.
- As part of your life-destiny, in every moment seek the answers to life's deepest questions, and in so doing, trust in your own greatness and that of the world around you.

- Most importantly, discover your truth in order to follow your path and purpose in life—in this moment and in every moment to come, without delay or restriction.

Last, but certainly not least, we cannot give up on human nature. Although we face skepticism and doubt, distrust, and disease around many corners, we must not give up on the potential and greatness of each and every one of us to stay true to our path and purpose. We must do our part to make this world everything it is destined to be, and more.

- We are all born equal; we all maintain the *potential* for greatness, but not the requirement.

We all have the potential for excellence in our blood and in our soul, but it is not a mandate: it is optional, a choice that must be made again and again in every moment throughout our lives. We can choose to be the person we were yesterday, or we can choose to reinvent ourselves in this very moment and in every one that follows.

- Staying true to our path and purpose in life is more than a commitment; it is a lifetime of action.

Around every turn we are tested and pushed, questioned and released, continually given the opportunity to make the right decision, to grow and to become the greatness within ourselves. Inside this every moment and every one that follows, we have been given the responsibility and the power to choose, and that is the greatest freedom in this world. Life really is so very simple at its core. All challenges, cycles, and realities are easily reduced to a simple understanding of the sequences within humanity. How we live and what we do are all elements of the life we have chosen, that we continue to choose every moment of every day. The past and the future exist only within our mind, for this very moment is the only one that exists.

- We must take responsibility for our choices and consciously choose life, greatness, and a path of excellence; it is the only destiny worthy of who we are.

About the Author

To thine own self be true.
—William Shakespeare

SOMETIMES WE ARE GIVEN DIRECTION AND GUIDANCE AS TO our path and purpose in life, yet we ignore it because we think *we* know what's best. I spent the majority of my life ignoring my own truth and path—only to suffer the consequences of my own ignorance and stubbornness.

I grew up in Albuquerque, New Mexico, and am the product of public education. Although I had some great teachers, my education left much to be desired. It was my parents who gave me the freedom and confidence to succeed, to fail, and to follow my own path—regardless of its outcome. Thanks to scholarships, I attended the University of New Mexico and studied engineering and music performance (xylophone and marimba) even though my true passion was business and marketing.

Before graduation, I moved to New York to intern for General Motors and then went to Australia to work at the company's Holden facility. It was in Australia at the Victoria University of Technology that I completed my bachelor's degree in international trade with minors in marketing and accounting.

As my journeys continued, I explored Guatemala and Mexico and eventually landed in Boulder, Colorado, where I began my first business, met my wife, and started my family. It was shortly after putting down roots that I was diagnosed with testicular cancer. Perhaps it was the prospect of my impending death and losing everything of meaning that inspired me to listen to my truth and write what my soul had been screaming to me all along. Eventually I was also diagnosed with thyroid cancer and I made the decision to simplify my life, which included selling a few of our companies, closing another, and focusing my energy on what was most important.

The material that would become the *Manual For Living* series poured from me uncontrollably for five years; even then it took another five years to prepare it for public consumption. The books contain both a rational explanation for life's experience as well as the truth of my soul and the universe as they relate to this physical existence.

The *Manual For Living* is more about your stories than mine, and I hope the information is as valuable to you as it has been to me. I share my story not to detail my uniqueness, but to demonstrate how similar our paths become as every action brings us one step closer to death. Throughout life, we are constantly challenged to become whole—to find our true purpose, to experience true happiness, to be of service, to listen to our truth, and to follow our path.

If I can leave you with one piece of wisdom: be true to yourself. It doesn't matter what anyone else thinks; this is your life and you are in the driver's seat. Hold onto your dreams, and never let *anyone* stand in the way of your path and what you truly desire.

I wish you the very best in your journey,

Many blessings!

—Seth David Chernoff

Acknowledgements

Don't compromise yourself. You're all you've got.
—Janis Joplin

HOW CAN ONE EVEN BEGIN TO ACKNOWLEDGE ALL OF THOSE who have touched our lives, who have played a role in our creation, in our refinement, in helping to shape us? We are the sum total of every opportunity, every decision, and every experience that has occurred thus far in our lives. Whether from those we love, those we hate, or even those we have never met, we have been shaped and formed by an infinite amount of input from all over the world, past and present, much of which we may have no conscious realization.

- We receive in ways impossible to fully comprehend, just as we give and serve where the end contribution is rarely seen nor fully understood.

Our opportunity is to acknowledge the endless contributions we receive in so many ways throughout all of our lives and to continue our commitment to improve not just the lives of those we love, but of our greater communities as well. We are forced to acknowledge every aspect of our world and community at large so that those we love are given equal credence to those we hate, even though we are ashamed to admit it. Those who hurt us the most, who have caused us unimaginable amounts of pain, suffering, and grief are many times the most significant contributors to our evolution, for they help to shape and define who we are and help us fully commit to our path and purpose in life.

There is an intricate balance, not only in our outside world but also internally, as we pay tribute to all of the centers of our being. We acknowledge all aspects of ourselves, our day-to-day involvements and commitments to act responsibly as working adults, parents, good friends, heads of households, and contributing members of our societies. Outside the world itself, we acknowledge those closest to our hearts on a moment-by-moment basis, whether our family, our friends, Spirit, or our faith, belief, or divine path, that provide all the input and guidance we require and desire. With divinity and judgment aside, all of the actors deserve their credit for the roles they play in guiding and helping us to see, learn, understand, evolve on a continual basis, and become the greatness to which each of us has been destined.

Thank you.,

Affirmation of Purpose

FEAR NOT, DEAR SOUL FOR YOUR WORRIES AND CONCERNS ARE not required. All preparations and reparations have preceded you; your physical body and spiritual presence is all that is required for the pace of humankind to progress into the greatness of time and the peace of timelessness. Breathe freely and embrace your sovereign soul through the heart of the universe while surpassing the intellect, for it is the heart that holds the key to the power within. Grow to the fullness of yourself and consciously determine your reality from the truth within, beyond the whims and passing of hope and desire. Follow your mind to where you follow your heart; create balance in reason, for your destiny is created before your very eyes. Step firmly, or the earth beneath your feet will crumble for lack of intention, purpose, and structure. The motion of progression is the action of a conscious reality created in the moment, of the moment, and for the moment.

~ Live free, for your freedom is the delimiter for which you search.

Step into the night, for when the sun sets it will call upon you for service of the deepest intention. Be assured that it will call upon your mind, your heart, and your soul as it continues to rise and fall. Take responsibility for the destiny before you, and accept the life of service before you, for it is why you are here.

~ All that you seek and all that you desire are here and ever present, simply for your choosing.

Highlights

- Every one of us is the hope of an undetermined future.
- Why do we force ourselves to suffer before we allow ourselves to evolve?
- By attempting to be right, we will sacrifice not only our relationships, but our life itself, for the basis for our life is the connections we share.
- Knowledge does not create wisdom; having all the right answers at the wrong time makes no one the wiser.
- Our goal in this lifetime is not to stake our claim, but to help manifest the connectedness in others that we innately seek within ourselves.
- We live a life that has no value, no meaning, and no purpose when it is incongruent with our inner truth.
- Decide carefully, for in this moment you are the person you choose to be.
- By choosing not to see what stands before us, we choose ignorance over evolution.
- Seldom is hatred as strong as when it is the result of two people who previously loved each other.
- Children teach us patience, understanding, trust, and allow us to experience the entire gamut of human emotion.

- We have been given ALL the gifts and tools needed to obtain all that we require.
- The healthier we get, the harder it is to keep sick people in our life.
- Children learn more from who we are than by what we say or attempt to teach or preach.
- Death supersedes all else when faced with the struggles of our existence.
- It is that which exists within us that allows us to operate outside of ourselves.
- Our world is in harmony when we can operate from a state of gratitude for that which we have and for that to which we aspire.
- We are superior to nobody, inferior to no one.
- What we truly desire cannot be obtained outside of ourselves.
- We make decisions that force us to perpetually sacrifice. As a result, we not only provide less of ourselves to our loved ones, we become less as a result.
- No matter what pain and suffering we incur as children, our decision to live this moment in the potentiality of the future is the only one we have.
- Blame is a poor excuse for not consciously choosing to live our magnificence.
- We are not seeking anything, for there is nothing to seek. All is here and now, in this precise moment.
- All of the answers we seek are held deep within our soul, simply waiting for us to reach for them.
- Remember, we can go anywhere from here . . .